LEADERSHIP AND MANAGEMENT OF RELIGIOUS ORGANIZATIONS

An Annotated Bibliography

Paul L. Golden, C.M., J.C.D.

Institute for Leadership of Religious Organizations
DePaul University
Chicago

Golden, Paul L., 1939-
    Leadership and management of religious organizations.

    Includes index.
    1. Christian leadership--Bibliography. 2. Church
management--Bibliography. I. DePaul University.
Institute for Leadership of Religious Organizations.
II. Title.
Z7781.G64 1989 [BV652.1]   016.262'1 88-82299

ISBN 0-9622747-0-4
Library of Congress Catalog Card Number: 88-82299

To order copies, contact:

DePaul University
Institute for Leadership of
  Religious Organizations
25 East Jackson Boulevard
Chicago, Illinois 60604-2287

Contents

PREFACE

This annotated bibliography was the first research project of the newly established Institute for Leadership of Religious Organizations. To my knowledge it is the only comprehensive annotated bibliography on leadership of religious organizations.

After reviewing existing bibliographies from libraries and other institutes, centers and programs on church leadership, there was a clear need for an extensive, inter-denominational annotated listing of available books on the topic. Other bibliographies were either limited to meet a specific need or were too inclusive of non-religious materials.

The search for relevant titles was mainly carried out by means of computerized data bases. The most important data bases were LE MARC and Religion Index. The other data bases used with limited success were Dissertation Abstracts, ABI Inform, Psychological Abstracts, ERIC and Sociological Abstracts.

Titles were included in this bibliography if they treated the theory and practice of administration, management and leadership of religious associations. Special attention was given to finding books which treat the theme of leadership from the theological and biblical perspective.

The focus of this bibliography is on the leaders of religious organizations. Leaders are those who are appointed or assume the role of director, supervisor, and decision-maker on behalf of a group, usually called parish, church or synagogue. Lay leadership or the leadership development of an individual church member is excluded from this work. Also excluded from this bibliography are books on general management theory or management of not-for-profit organizations. Finally, titles which treat of some particular church or pastoral situation were included if the information could be generalized.

Emphasis was placed on more recent titles. However titles dating back to 1960 were also included if the book had material which seems relevant today or is considered a classic work. There are no titles published after 1987.

The annotations describe the contents of the book. Every effort was made to help the reader know the background and experience of the author(s), the theological principles underlying the work and the practical skills discussed. No attempt was made to evaluate or pass judgement on the work.

This annotated bibliography was made possible because of the dedication and expertise of many people. I am grateful to Mr. Martin Pimsler who served as the library researcher. He organized and directed the computer searches and maintained records of all the books which were ordered from the libraries around the region. Ms. Margaret Power and the entire library staff at the Lincoln Park campus of DePaul were very cooperative. Sr. Jane Gerard, CSJ, my Administrative Assistant, edited and formatted the text and prepared it for publication.

The funds for the initial phase of this project were generously awarded by the DePaul University Research Council.

Finally, I would like to express my gratitude for the Advisory Board of the Institute for Leadership for its guidance and encouragement in this project and in the other programs of the Institute.

Paul L. Golden, C.M.
Director
Institute for Leadership

February, 1989

CHAPTER ONE

Business Administration

ATKINSON, C. Harry. *How To Get Your Church Built.* Garden City: Doubleday, 1964. 217pp.

The purpose of this book, says the author, "is to state simply and briefly some of the current thinking in church circles which carries with it far-reaching implications for the religious architecture of today and tomorrow." After some chapters on introduction and principles, he writes a chapter on each of the main spaces found in a church. The book concludes with chapters on color and light, choosing an architect, selecting a site, raising funds and christian art. There are numerous photos and drawings throughout the work.

BRAMER, John C., Jr. *Efficient Church Business Management.* Philadelphia: Westminster Press, 1960. 150pp.

This basic book in business management is a combination of theory and practice. It explains the needs and principles of budgeting, reporting, accounting, purchasing, and setting wage schedules. It also gives practical examples and illustrations in each area. There is an extensive bibliography at the end of the book.

De THOMASIS, Louis. *My Father's Business: Creating a New Future for the People of God.* Westminster, MD: Christian Classics, 1984. 167pp.

Convinced that the church can benefit from the insights of business management, the author argues that a major obstacle to introducing these insights is the strong resistance to any type of management in the ministry. The book presents and summarizes many of the major classical and contemporary contributions to the art and science of management. It will serve as a primer for those engaged in church administration. (From a review by Kevin Sullivan).

DITZEN, Lowell Russell. *Handbook of Church Administration.* New York: MacMillan, 1962. 390pp.

This volume summarizes the author's many years as a pastor and administrator in the Presbyterian Church. He has outlined the main tasks and functions of a church leader and collected information which clearly shows that a pastor is also a manager of a "business". The book emphasizes the central role of lay people in administration.

DUNKIN, Steve. *Church Advertising.* Nashville: Abingdon Press, 1982. 126pp.

The author discusses the theory and practice of advertising for new church members. He uses examples from his pastorate of Chippewa Presbyterian Church in New York. The chapters treat such topics as creating an advertising strategy, building a church image, using newspapers, using radio and setting an advertising budget.

FELDMAN, Julian. *Church Purchasing Procedures.* Englewood Cliffs: Prentice Hall, 1964. 192pp.

Churches purchase both goods and services. This book explains effective organization for church purchasing. The merits of centralizing the purchasing functions and the selection of sources and choice of supplier. The author provides forms and methods for making requisitions, getting competitive bids, inventory controls and replacing equipment. Finally there are sections on warranties, tax exemption and fraud.

GRAY, Robert N. *Church Business Administration: An Emerging Profession.* Enid, OK: Phillips University Press, 1968. 116pp.

This booklet describes the need and functions of a church business administration. In short and well-focused chapters, it treats the developing need for this kind of management, the job of the business manager, and the kind of person who would be best in the job. The last chapter speaks about growth in professionalism in this area. The appendices reprint various documents approved by the National Association of Church Business Administrators.

KNUDSEN, Raymond B. *New Models for Church Administration: The Practical Application of Business Principles.* Chicago: Association Press, 1979. 165pp.

This is the third in a series of new models books which the author applies to the adminsitration of the local church. After introducing the book with a chapter comparing the common elements of business and religion, he treats long-range planning, funding, budgeting, stewardship, staffing and leadership.

LINAMEN, Harold F. *Business Handbook for Churches.* Anderson, IN: Warner Press, 1957. 176pp.

Dr Linamen taught business education at Anderson College and was a partner in an accounting firm. He has written about the essential aspects of the business life of a church. He treats incorporation, running meetings, personnel, insurance, investments, real estate, remodeling, fund-raising, bookkeeping, budgets, public relations and legal issues.

MYERS, Marvin F., comp. *Managing the Business Affairs of the Church.* Nashville: Convention Press, 1981. 144pp.

This manual is a basic guide related to the full range of church business affairs. It treats personnel, salaries, budgeting, management, computers, insurance, investments, taxes and church property maintenance. Each chapter is written by a person experienced in that area. All authors are affiliated with the Baptist church.

NEITHOLD, Eugene C. *Church Business Policies Outlined.* Greenville, SC: Church Books, 1976. 176pp.

This book is a collection of suggested policies and their related forms for church business procedures. The author offers them as starting points for a church which needs to formalize its own business policies and forms. The second section has thirteen accounting procedures and forms. All policies, procedures and forms appear as typed on an IBM Selectric so a pastor can visualize their final appearance.

ODOM, Randall Young. *A Study of Environment, Strategy and Planning Processes in Churches.* Unpublished Ph.D. dissertation: University of Mississippi, 1984.

This is the author's dissertation for the Ph.D. in Business Administration. "The purpose of the study was to determine if churches pursue strategies and to investigate the relationship between strategies, organizational environments, and the extent of planning completeness and sophistication within church organizations" (p 21). The author surveyed literature on planning and strategy models. He surveyed churches in the Arkansas Baptist State Convention.

OWENSBY, Idus V. *Church Custodian's Manual.* Nashville: Convention Press, 1974. 48pp.

This is a practical manual on the job and tools of a custodian. It uses cartoons and outline form to deliver its message.

PHILLIPS, Harold R. and Robert E. Firth. *Cases in Denominational Administration: A Management Casebook for Decision-making.* Berrier Springs, MI: Andrews University Press, 1978. 314pp.

As the title indicates, this book is a collection of cases chosen to show the kinds of problems with which church administrators must grapple. The cases are grouped in the following sections: church institutions, church operated commercial enterprises, conference organizations, local churches and pastoral problems and personal and personnel problems. The last two sections will appeal to seminars, study groups and classes. The first section focuses more on decisions to be made in business related situations. The book begins with two chapters explaining how to analyze a case.

SMITH, H. Paul and Ezra Earl Jones. *The Church Building Process.* Cincinnati: United Methodist Development Fund, 1975. 39pp.

The purpose of this booklet is to provide an overview of steps to be followed in building a church. Detailed information is not provided. There is information on preliminary planning, site selection, choosing an architect, construction and financing. The authors are experienced pastoral administrators.

TAYLOR, Robert C. *How To Maintain Your Church Buildings and Grounds.* Westwood, NJ: Fleming H. Revell Co, 1962. 63pp.

A past officer of the American Society for Church Architecture, the author has served as designer and consultant for a number of new and renovated churches. He writes from his experience about how to set up a program of maintenance for churches. He treats the topics of record keeping, inventory and inspection, financial planning, project timing and delegation.

WALZ, Edgar. *Church Business Methods.* St. Louis: Concordia Publishing House, 1970. 85pp.

In this handbook of methods for effective management of church business, the author, a busines manager and professor of psychology, treats such topics as organization, supervision, the church office, church records, financial reports, building maintenance and legal issues.

WILLIAMS, Denny. *Leadership Life-Style.* Kansas City, MO: Beacon Hill Press, 1983. 120pp.

The author, an ordained minister and a doctor of business administration, explains the basic principles of staff management. He directs his writing to the pastor and others who have positions of leadership in the local church. This volume is divided into six main headings. Each heading contains many topics which cover, on average, two pages. Every aspect of parish administration, organization, personnel service, advertising and office management is treated in practical fashion.

CHAPTER TWO

Case Studies

ANDERSON, James D. *To Come Alive!* San Francisco: Harper & Row, 1973. 141pp.

The author, a church planner, shares what he has learned about member motivation, sources of power, utilizatiion of conflict, leadership and management of change. A blend of theology and behavioral science theory, this book is filled with examples and case studies. It offers practical suggestions to reorganize congregational structures.

BAXTER, Nathan Dwight. *Four Cases and Teaching Resources to Enable Religious Leaders to be More Subjectively and Theoretically Aware in Parish Conflict Situations.* Unpublished D.Min. Dissertation: Lancaster Theological Seminary, 1985. 183pp.

This Doctor of Ministry dissertation contains four case studies in the subject of conflict in the parish. The areas of conflict are: negotiating for self-interest; parish community relations; organizational subsystems; pastoral care. After each case there is a section on teaching the case and a section on goals and resources.

DEEGAN, Arthur X. *The Priest As Manager.* New York: The Bruce Publishing Co, 1969. 154pp.

For this author the manager is the coordinator of the activities of others. The functions of a manager are planning, organizing, directing, motivating and controlling. This book aims to help the priest be more effective as an administrative leader. It discusses the process of management and the development of management theory. It explains the use of time, the art of delegation, styles of leadership, management by objectives and problem solving. The author concludes the book with a case study.

DUDLEY, Carl S., ed. *Building Effective Ministry: Theory and Practice in the Local Church.* San Francisco: Harper & Row, 1983. 267pp.

The purpose of this collection of essays is to provide new avenues into the social and spiritual dynamics of a local church. The book is a series of reflections on a "case". The first set of reflections are written from the vantage point of academic disciplines. The next set, from the point of view of church consultants. The final set of reflections attempts to integrate the various approaches.

GOODMAN, Grace A. *Rocking the Ark.* New York: United
Presbyterian Church, 1968. 214pp.

These nine case studies demonstrate how some churches have
renewed themselves. These cases were first used during a series
of consultations conducted by the Division of Evangelism of the
Presbyterian Church. Each case studies a church of different size
and different environment. The author concludes the book with
questions and her observations.

LEAS, Speed B. *Time Management.* Nashville: Abingdon, 1978. 123pp.

This volume explains how church leaders must take the initiative
if they are to be good stewards of the hours given by God to them.
A good leader cannot passively accept the demands placed by
others. The leader must set priorities and allocate time. The author
does not simply list "oughts" but the "laws" to use time creatively
and effectively. The compulsive worker and the procrastinator are
described and used as case studies.

LEWIS, G. Douglass. *Resolving Church Conflicts: A Case Study Approach
For Local Congregations.* New York: Harper and Row, 1981. 182pp.

The purpose of this book is to aid individuals and institutions in
becoming more effective managers of conflict. It is based on the
belief that all of us have or can develop the capacity to experience
and use conflict so that it becomes a stimulation to our growth
and development. The author designed the volume so that it
moves from theory toward practice. There is a series of cases
which serve as the link from theory to practice.

LUECKE, David S. and Samuel Southard. *Pastoral Administration.*
Waco: Word Books, 1986. 207pp.

The subtitle of this volume is: Integrating Ministry and
Management in the Church. The authors have chosen six areas of
pastoral experience. One begins the chapter with a case study and
proceeds to pull out the principles and pastoral practice at work.
The other author concludes the chapter with his comments and
reflections. The areas treated are management issues in a pastoral
setting.

MICKEY, Paul A. and Robert L. Wilson. *Conflict and Resolution.* Nashville: Abingdon, 1973. 160pp.

This book uses case studies to examine the issues of conflict between individuals and groups in the church. After a chapter on the theological and psychological principles of conflict, there is a series of short case studies with discussion questions designed to highlight the basic issues involved. No decisions or solutions are offered.

PHILLIPS, Harold R. and Robert E. Firth. *Cases in Denominational Administration: A Management Casebook for Decision-making.* Berrier Springs, MI: Andrews University Press, 1978. 314pp.

As the title indicates, this book is a collection of cases chosen to show the kinds of problems with which church administrators must grapple. The cases are grouped in the following sections: church institutions, church operated commercial enterprises, conference organizations, local churches and pastoral problems and personal and personnel problems. The last two sections will appeal to seminars, study groups and classes. The first section focuses more on decisions to be made in business related situations. The book begins with two chapters explaining how to analyze a case.

RUDGE, Peter F. *Management in the Church.* London: McGraw Hill, 1976. 172pp.

In the first section of this book the author establishes the relevance of management in the church. A case is made in each of the various fields of management (personnel, financial, property, household, office, time) and the case is argued on a very practical level. The second section describes new intiatives for restructuring the church, using examples from the Catholic Church. It is then demonstrated that this new church idiom bears close resemblance to management concepts found in the business world.

SAFRANSKI, Scott R. *Managing God's Organization: The Catholic Church in Society.* Ann Arbor., MI: UMI Research Press, 1985. 199pp.

This volume is the revision of the author's doctoral dissertation. It studies the Catholic Church from an organizational, not theological perspective. The focus is the interaction of units, at various levels of the church's hierarchy, with groups outside the church. Church organization and management processes are then studied in terms of adaptations made in an effort to assume cooperation and stable relationships with important internal and external interest groups and resource suppliers. The work contains the results of an empirical case study in which the resource dependence model was applied to one archdiocese.

SCHALLER, Lyle E. *Planning for Protestantism in Urban America.* Nashville: Abingdon, 1965. 217pp.

This book is written from the perspective that planning is a process in which everyone who has a voice as a decision maker participates. The author begins with a case study. He then treats external assumptions, the theology of planning, planning interdenominationally, inner city planning and urban planning for churches.

WALRATH, Douglas A. *Leading Churches Through Change.* Nashville: Abingdon, 1979. 124pp.

This is a collection of six case studies of churches and change. In each case the author explains the problem, the solution and applications to other situations. The author is a church development consultant who formerly served as an executive with the Reformed Church in America.

CHAPTER THREE

Finances and Budgeting

ALLRED, Thurman W. *Basic Small Church Administration*. Nashville: Convention Press, 1981. 64pp.

This is a practical "how-to" book aimed at pastors of small, rural churches having Southern Baptist affiliation. The authors are mostly experienced pastors who discuss skills such as administration, programming, decision-making, planning and budgeting.

BRAMER, John C., Jr. *Efficient Church Business Management*. Philadelphia: Westminster Press, 1960. 150pp.

This basic book in business management is a combination of theory and practice. It explains the needs and principles of budgeting, reporting, accounting, purchasing, and setting wage schedules. It also gives practical examples and illustrations in each area. There is an extensive bibliography at the end of the book.

CLAGETT, John Y. *Management for the Self-Governing Church.* Buffalo Grove, IL: J.Y. Clagett, 1983. 151pp.

Leaders in self-governing churches who are not confident with their role desciptions will find much practical advice in this book. It covers such topics as planning, budgeting, managing time, decision-making, motivation and training other leaders.

COLE, Harper L. *Handling Finances in the Local Church*. Kansas City, MO: Beacon Hill Press, 1966. 96pp.

Designed as a manual and workbook for those who are responsible for church finances, it has been used as a text in the seminary. This practical booklet explains all areas of receiving funds, disbursements, accounting and budgeting. The last chapter consists of practice problems.

HOLCK, Manfred, Jr. *Accounting Methods for the Small Church*. Minneapolis: Augsburg, 1961. 108pp.

"This manual seeks to provide information for the church officer on the best way to keep accurate financial records. It outlines a bare minimum in financial records for the small church. It suggests the best business-like approach and promotes uniformity and accuracy. Some recommended accounting methods for the small church are illustrated." (From the introduction). The author has provided many sample forms, illustrations and a glossary.

HOLCK, Manfred, Jr. *Annual Budgeting: Developing and Using an Annual Budget Effectively.* Minneapolis: Augsburg, 1977. 46pp.

Based on the premise that an annual budget can make the church's management of resources more effective, the author outlines procedures for developing and using an annual budget. This booklet explains the nature of a budget, the various kinds of budgets and how to develop one. The practicality of this work is shown by its numerous illustrations.

HOLCK, Manfred, Jr. *Cash Management: Stewardship of the Church's Cash Resources.* Minneapolis: Augsburg, 1978. 40pp.

This short treatise is a practical handbook on cash management for churches. It covers principles, procedures, investing, banking and borrowing. It is replete with illustrations.

HOLCK, Manfred, Jr. *Church Finance in a Complex Economy: Financing the Church, a Changing Strategy in a Changing Economy.* Nashville: Abingdon, 1983. 128pp.

This book is about the impact that inflation has on the church's financial resources. After explaining the ways inflation affects resources, the author treats several methods for countering the impact of inflation.

HOLCK, Manfred, Jr. *Payroll Tax Procedures for Churches and Clergy and How Clergy Report Income to IRS.* Austin: Church Management, 1985. 30pp.

Effective January 1, 1984, all congregations were required to withhold social security taxes and pay the employer social security tax on all wages paid to all full-time and part-time employees (except clergy) who earned at least $100 during the year. This booklet, authored by the well-known CPA and published by THE CLERGY JOURNAL, explains the new law and gives sample forms.

HOLCK, Manfred, Jr. and Manfred Holck, Sr. *Complete Handbook of Church Accounting*. Englewood Cliffs, NJ: Prentice-Hall, 1978. 300pp.

These authors, father and son, have written extensively on the theme of church finances and money management. This volume is truly a practical handbook which will enable its reader to keep proper financial records and report them to the church membership in an understandable fashion. Because the accounting profession has never really defined "accepted" accounting principles for churches, the authors present the best principles from several methods, while aiming for ease and precision.

HOLT, David R. *Handbook of Church Finance*. New York: Macmillan, 1960. 201pp.

Few areas of the church's life are more obscure than financial administration of the Lord's work. There has been interest in producing a body of sound stewardship literature based on a biblical understanding of divine ownership and the resultant cosmic relationship of God's people to God's property. The purpose of this study is to gather and report the results of a questionnaire on the need for a handbook in church finance and to write such a handbook. (From the Introduction).

KATZ, Irving I. and Myron E. Schoen. *Successful Synagogue Administration*. New York: Union of American Hebrew Congregations, 1963. 200pp.

This is a manual of administration for the synagogue leader. It is addressed to rabbis, cantors, educators as well as professional administrators and lay committeepersons. It treats such issues as the board of trustees, committee structure, finances, maintenance, membership and the synagogue office.

KNUDSEN, Raymond B. *Models for Ministry: Creative Administration in the Local Church*. New York: Friendship Press, 1978. 98pp.

The author, a United Presbyterian pastor, is the director of the National Consultation on Financial Development. This book, one of several in church leadership, collects his experiences and ideas on church management. It treats such topics as interpersonal communication skills, program development, use of facilities and space, scheduling, finances and goal setting.

KNUDSEN, Raymond B. *New Models for Church Administration: The Practical Application of Business Principles*. Chicago: Association Press, 1979. 165pp.

This is the third in a series of new models books which the author applies to the administration of the local church. After introducing the book with a chapter comparing the common elements of business and religion, he treats long-range planning, funding, budgeting, stewardship, staffing and leadershipp.

MAVIS, W. Curry. *Advancing . . . the Smaller Church*. Grand Rapids: Baker Book House, 1968. 180pp.

The author writes about the urban and rural church with fewer than 150 members. He discusses principles which underlie effective work in these churches. He treats such topics as planning, organizing, budgeting, public relations, worship and education.

MYERS, Marvin F., comp. *Managing the Business Affairs of the Church*. Nashville: Convention Press, 1981. 144pp.

This manual is a basic guide related to the full range of church business affairs. It treats personnel, salaries, budgeting, management, computers, insurances, investments, taxes and church property maintenance. Each chapter is written by a person experienced in that area. All authors are affliated with the Baptist church.

PAGE, Harry Robert. *Church Budget Development*. Englewood Cliffs, NJ: Prentice-Hall, 1964. 192pp.

This book aims at increasing effectiveness in planning and controlling the financial resources of the individual church. Budget development and use are treated as an administrative process common to churches of all denominations and sizes. This volume describes the underlying purposes of budgeting, its advantages and limitations, and its relationship to programs and future plans of the church. The entire budgeting process is explained and various techniques are explored. (Author's preface).

PETERSON, Robert E. *Handling the Church's Money*. St. Louis: Bethany Press, 1965. 61pp.

This small handbook provides an overall view of the financial responsibilities of a church. It outlines the jobs of the church treasurer and the financial secretary. There are many suggestions for efficient job performance and methods of bookkeeping and report writing. Sample forms are also included.

POWELL, Luther P. *Money and the Church*. Chicago: Association Press, 1962. 252pp.

The author had two purposes in writing this book: to trace the various motives and methods throughout history of the christian church and to set forth some guiding principles for financing the church today. Part one discusses history up to the Reformation. Part two treats the church in early America. The last part focuses on the present time.

SCHALLER, Lyle E. *Effective Church Planning*. Nashville: Abingdon, 1979. 176pp.

This book is intended to assist the pastor in problem-solving. The basic assumption in these pages is that people can resolve problems well if they have an accurate diagnosis of the nature of the situation. The author teaches how to identify and deal with the underlying factors which have low visibility but high impact on the dynamics of parish life. From this perspective the book deals with worship space, budgeting, evangelism, tenure and fellowship.

STILES, Joseph. *Acquiring and Developing Church Real Estate*. Englewood Cliffs: Prentice-Hall, 1965. 189pp.

This book treats the topic of purchasing and developing property for the use of a local congregation. It explains the necessary steps of appointing a building commitee, studying and planning, working with an architect, fund-raising and other topics. The author, a businessman and university professor, was director of the Center for Church Business Management.

United Methodist Church. *Guidelines for Leadership in the Local Church.* Nashville: Abingdon, 1984.

This is a series of thirty booklets which provide guidance for leaders of local churches. The booklets treat such topics as administrative boards, role of the pastor, finances, mission and each ministry of the church. The booklet describes the topic and how it is to be organized. These guidelines were prepared by the Interagency Task Force on Resources of the United Methodist Church.

WALKER, Arthur L. *Church Accounting Methods.* Englewood Cliffs: Prentice-Hall, 1964. 170pp.

"This handbook is addressed to all those persons who are concerned with making and maintaining financial records for churches and their related organizations. Its purpose is to serve as a guide to those who design and keep a well-ordered system of financial accounts for churches." (from the Preface). This volume is designed so that a person with little or no formal training can learn through study. There are over thirty illustrations not counting the two appendices.

WHEELEY, B. Otto and T. Cable. *Church Planning and Management.* Philadelphia: Dorrance and Co, 1975. 218pp.

The authors, industrial executives and members of Baptist congregations, write about the basic principles of management applied to all protestant churches. The volume is a handbook for local congregations. The chapters on planning, organization, constitutions, finances, education, recreation, worship and promotional methods are general, practical and accompanied by charts.

CHAPTER FOUR

Fund-raising and Stewardship

ANDERSON, Arthur and Co. *Tax Economics of Charitable Giving,* 9th
ed. Chicago: Arthur Andersen & Co, 1985. 215pp.

This new edition continues to give information about tax benefits
to those who make gifts to charity. Besides gifts of money, this
book treats the tax benefits of securities, life insurance, property,
antiques, etc. This is not a stewardship book, but as the title
indicates, a tax book. (From a review by Manfred Holck, Jr.).

BRATTGORD, Helge. *God's Stewards: A Theological Study of the
Principles of Stewardship.* Trans. by Gene J. Lund. Minneapolis:
Augsburg, 1963. 248pp.

The first half of this book examines the notion of stewardship in
the scriptures. The second half analyzes the Lutheran confessions
for a theology of stewardship. As a result of his study, the author,
a Swedish theologian and minister, believes that stewardship is
more than fund-raising. It is the care of all gifts given by God.

BRIGGS, Edwin A., ed. *Theological Perspectives of Stewardship.*
Evanston, Il: United Methodist Church, 1969. 165pp.

In the spring of 1967 a seminar on stewardship was held in
Chicago. The Stewardship and Finance section of the United
Methodist Church designed the seminar as a study to provide
background for the formulation of a creed or foundation
statement. The twelve lectures of the seminar form the chapters
of this book.

CARLSON, Martin E. *Why People Give.* New York: National Council
of Churches, 1968. 174pp.

The theme of this book is motivation in Christian giving.
Questions raised and answered are: what is money? why does a
person give? what is Chistian giving? what part does faith play in
motivation?, and what implications do these reflections have on
stewardship. This book was written for the pastor and the
stewardship lay leaders.

CUNNINGHAM, Richard B. *Creative Stewardship*. Nashville: Abingdon, 1979. 128pp.

This little book contains guidelines for applying principles and patterns of christian stewardship. The author, associate professor of Christian Philosophy at Southern Baptist Theological Seminary, begins with the scriptural and theological meanings of stewardship. He then describes the process of good stewardship and ends with some thoughts on the corporate stewardship of the Church.

De MENA, Henry F., Jr. *How to Increase Parish Income*. Mystic, CT: Twenty-third Publications, 1982 132+pp.

This 'how-to' manual gives detailed instructions for all types of parish fund-raising: capital campaign, offertory collections, tithing, borrowing from members, etc. It contains sample forms and homey suggestions. The author reflects his knowledge and experience in the Catholic Church.

ESPIE, John C. and Thomas C. Rieke. *Opportunities in Stewardship*. Nashville: Discipleship Resources, 1975. 148pp.

The authors have served as directors of conference stewardship programs within the United Methodist Church. They believe that church stewardship must embrace more than a single annual fund-raising event. This book clarifies the meaning of stewardship, describes specific programs for raising money and looks toward what is possible in the future.

HALL, Douglas John. *The Steward: A Biblical Symbol Come of Age*. New York: Friendship Press for the Commission of Stewardship, NCC, 1982. 147pp.

This book provides the biblical background necessary to rethink, in the light of our contemporary situation, the origins of the idea of christian stewardship. This is done through reflection on the historical evolution of North American Church practice as it incorporated stewardship into its life and work. The author, a professor of Christian Theology at McGill University in Montreal, believes that we had lost the original meaning of stewardship. It is not a function of mission but mission is a function of stewardship! (From the bookjacket).

HARRELL, Costen J. *Stewardship and the Tithe.* New York: Abingdon, 1953. 61pp.

This book treats the christian doctrine of stewardship by addressing three issues: the biblical basis of stewardship, the theological teaching and the history and practice of tithing. The author indicated only a few of his sources.

HEYD, Thomas. *Planning for Stewardship.* Minneapolis: Augsburg, 1980. 40pp.

This is a practical book about developing a giving program for church congregations; after explaining the biblical meaning of stewardship, the author treats planning and organizing a stewardship program. There are five pages of exhibits.

HOLCK, Manfred, Jr. *Cash Management: Stewardship of the Church's Cash Resources.* Minneapolis: Augsburg, 1978. 40pp.

This short treatise is a practical handbook on cash management for churches. It covers principles, procedures, investing, banking and borrowing. It is replete with illustrations.

HOLCK, Manfred, Jr. *Money and Your Church: How to Raise More, How to Manage It Better.* New Canaan, CT: Keats Publishing Co, 1974. 189pp.

This is a practical approach to raising and managing money in the local church. Mr Holck discusses first where the money is to come from. He then writes about what motivates a person to give. He sets out a solid plan, with concrete examples, for a successful fund drive. Finally the author presents information on will programs, life insurance, tax deductions, deferred gifts and endowments.

HOLLOWAY, George T., ed. *Bibliography of Fund-raising and Philanthropy.* Rockville Centre: National Catholic Development Conference, 1982. 76pp.

The NCDC is the nation's largest professional association of fund-raising organizations. This unannotated bibliography covers such topics as the arts, corporate giving, foundations, hospitals, tax and legal issues and techniques of fund-raising.

HOLT, David R. *Handbook of Church Finance.* New York: Macmillan, 1960. 201pp.

Few areas of the church's life are more obscure than financial administration of the Lord's work. There has been interest in producing a body of sound stewardship literature based on a biblical understanding of divine ownership and the resultant cosmic relationship of God's people to God's property. The purpose of this study is to gather and report the results of a questionnaire on the need for a handbook in church finance and to write such a handbook. (From the Introduction).

KANTONEN, T. A. *A Theology for Christian Stewardship.* Philadelphia: The Muhlenberg Press, 1956. 126pp.

Stewardship is not merely money nor maintenance. It is vital christian faith in action. The author set out to write a concise but comprehensive summary of all major doctrines of Evangelical theology viewed in the perspective of their bearing on stewardship. Using the New Testament as a primary source, he used Luther as the guide to the heart of the gospel.

KNUDSEN, Raymond B. *New Models for Church Administration: The Practical Application of Business Principles.* Chicago: Association Press, 1979. 165pp.

This is the third in a series of new models books which the author applies to the administration of the local church. After introducing the book with a chapter comparing the common elements of business and religion, he treats long-range planning, funding, budgeting, stewardship, staffing and leadership.

KNUDSEN, Raymond B. *New Models for Financing the Local Church: Fresh Approaches to Giving in the Computer Age.* New York: Association Press, 1974. 157pp.

The author penned this book while serving as Assistant General Secretary for Donor Support for the National Council of Churches. He states five premises for his opinion that new models of financing are needed. He then writes about the models: every member canvass, project support, mail solicitation, grants, annuities, charitable remainder trust, life insurance, wills and bequests, and bank cards.

KUNTZ, Kenneth. *Wooden Chalices.* St. Louis: Bethany Press, 1963. 192pp.

This book on christian stewardship was written at the request of the stewardship committee of the Disciples of Christ Church. It is a collation of biblical passages, illustrations from literature and experience of the major experts of stewardship. It is intended as a resource for those who are required to give talks on this topic. The chapters of the book are written in the style of a meditation.

PETRY, Ronald D. *Partners in Creation: Stewardship for Pastor and People.* Elgin, IL: Brethren Press, 1980. 126pp.

This volume was designed as a text for a seminary course in stewardship. The first section treats the scriptural and theological dimensions of stewardship. The second section deals with the practical aspects from the point of view of the pastor. In one of the appendices, the author outlines a seven session study course entitled "a faith view of Stewardship". The author is a pastor of the Church of the Brethren.

POOVEY, W. A. *How to Talk to Christians about Money.* Minneapolis: Augsburg, 1982. 128pp.

This book is divided into two parts. The first discusses various aspects of stewardship. The second part contains short addresses on money based on various biblical texts. It is intended to assist the minister in speaking about money and stewardship.

SHEDD, Charlie W. *How To Develop a Tithing Church.* Nashville: Abingdon, 1961. 123pp.

This little book is a practical guide to tithing. It gives the history and theology of this kind of stewardship. It details a plan of operation and gives sample statements for the church bulletin and sample sermons.

THOMPSON, T. K., ed. *Stewardship in Contemporary Life.* New York: Association Press, 1965. 190pp.

Four authors write on the general theme of stewardship. The theme is approached from the viewpoint of scripture, ethics and corporate responsibility. Most of these chapters were first given as lectures at the workshop on Benevolence Promotion sponsored by the National Council of Churches in London, Ontario in 1964.

THOMPSON, Thomas K., ed. *Stewardship in Contemporary Theology.* New York: Association Press, 1980. 252pp.

This book is an outgrowth of a Theological Study Conference on Stewardship held in 1979 at Wagner College in New York. The conference was sponsored by the National Council of Churches. The nine chapters of this volume are the presentations made during the conference. The topics are: stewardship in the bible, history of christian stewardship, the theology of stewardship, tithing, and ethics of stewardship.

VAN BENSCHOTEN, A. Q., Jr. *What the Bible Says about Stewardship.* Valley Forge: Judson Press, 1983. 96pp.

This is a study guide book. It is designed for five two-hour study groups and includes a leader's guide. The author, the associate director for World Mission Support of the American Baptist Churches, primarily focuses on the bible and its practical application in daily life. God has given us stewardship over the world's resources and this program assists people in understanding God's plan.

WALKER, Joe W. *Money in the Church.* Nashville: Abingdon, 1982. 125pp.

"I believe talking about money in the church is holy talk, deeply theological, and as sacred as prayer." So says the author of this volume which examines the part money plays in the United Methodist Church. He reports on the past and present patterns of giving. He studies the motivation used in collecting money and the motives which move Methodists to give. The book concludes with a discussion of the financial pressures facing the denomination and offers some methods to meet these challenges.

CHAPTER FIVE

Group Dynamics and Communication

ADAMS, Jay E. *Shepherding God's Flock.* Grand Rapids: Baker Book House, 1979. 530pp.

This is three books in one volume. The first section on pastoral life treats the practical questions about the ministry such as making house calls, visiting the sick, managing time, etc. The second section is on pastoral counseling. The third section is on pastoral leadership. In it the author discusses his views of authority, delegation, communication, planning, program design, finance and other administrative topics.

ANDERSON, Philip A. *Church Meetings That Matter.* Philadelphia, Boston: United Church Press, 1965. 111+pp.

In nine short chapters, the author explores and explains the nature, purpose and process of successful groups. He treats the roles of leader and member as well as the process of evaluation.

BAXTER, Nathan Dwight. *Four Cases and Teaching Resources to Enable Religious Leaders to be More Subjectively and Theoretically Aware in Parish Conflict Situations.* Unpublished D.Min. Dissertation: Lancaster Theological Seminary, 1985. 183pp.

This Doctor of Ministry dissertation contains four case studies on the subject of conflict in the parish. The areas of conflict are: negotiating for self-interest; parish community relations; organizational subsystems; pastoral care. After each case there is a section on teaching the case and a section on goals and resources.

BELL, A. Donald. *How to Get Along with People in the Church.* Grand Rapids: Zondervan, 1960. 159pp.

The author believes that many church leaders are ineffective because they cannot get along with other people. He holds that there are three main sources of help for Christians with personality problems: the examples of Christ, the principles of applied psychology and the psychology of salesmanship. This book explains these sources and applies them to the church worker. Dr. Bell is professor of Psychology and Human Relations at Southwestern Baptist Theological Seminary. (From a review by A. Haze).

BORMANN, Ernest and Nancy Bormann. *Effective Committees and Groups in the Church.* Minneapolis: Augsburg, 1973. 104pp.

This is a practical book about groups in the church. The authors apply communication theory to the experience of various kinds of committees and groups. The work is divided into three areas: group dynamics, leadership and small group communication.

BOSSART, Donald E. *Creative Conflict in Religious Education and Church Administration.* Birmingham, AL: Religious Education Press, 1980. 284pp.

Acknowledging the reality of conflict in our churches, the author addresses the methods of using it for productive purposes. He explains the principles as well as some specific procedures for utilizing conflict to enhance religious education and church administration.

BREEN, David P. *Churches in Conflict: A Conflict Management Manual for Church Leaders.* Unpublished D.Min. dissertation: Western Theological Seminary, 1983. 134pp.

This four-unit manual is designed for church leaders as a guide to conflict management in the local congregation. It discusses a theory of organizational conflict and reports the results of a survey of church leaders in the Reformed Church of America on their responses to conflict. The manual explores the relationship between certain emotions and conflict and offers some scriptural and theological themes as resources.

BROWN, J. Truman. *Church Planning a Year at a Time.* Nashville: Convention Press, 1984. 24pp.

This booklet is a practical guide to church planning. It contains very little theory. There are numerous charts, timelines and questions which a planning group could use in its work.

CASTEEL, John L., ed. *The Creative Role of Interpersonal Groups in the Church Today.* New York: Association Press, 1968. 221pp.

This collection of essays covers the various kinds of growth groups found in churches today. The author intends to show new developments in group theory and to report on a variety of group experiences.

CUMMINGS, H. Wayland and Charles Somerville. *Overcoming Communication Barriers in the Church*. Valley Forge, PA: Judson, 1981. 175pp.

The authors, one an ordained Presbyterian minister and the other a professor of communications, have written this book out of conviction that communication is a serious problem faced by religious leaders. They focus on the practical aspects of communication-information exchange, problem-solving, conflict resolution, and changing behavior with a 'how-to-do-it' approach based on the research findings of social science.

DALE, Robert D. *Surviving Difficult Church Members*. Nashville: Abingdon, 1984. 126pp.

Each local church has its share of people whom most members find difficult to get along with in a satisfying manner. The author has grouped these people into six categories. After a chapter describing a difficult church member there is a chapter on the ministry skills necessary for effective congregational work with that personality type.

DITTES, James E. *When the People Say No*. San Francisco: Harper and Row, 1979. 150pp.

The author, an ordained minister of the United Church of Christ, addresses the question of the congregation's opposition to the pastor. What is a pastor to do when the people are uncooperative and angry? In seven chapters, the author addresses the issues of frustration and pain which the minister feels and offers solutions which help both the pastor and the congregation.

DOUTY, Mary Alice. *How To Work with Church Groups*. Nashville: Abingdon Press, 1957. 170pp.

This book attempts to put principles of group work and of democratic group leadership into practical terms. It is written for the church group leader or teacher. There are chapters on evaluating groups, group patterns, group organization, understandings, procedure, and techniques for good group functioning. There are chapters treating the specific concerns of groups in the church-school program.

HALL, Douglas T. and Benjamin Schneider. *Organizational Climates and Careers: The Work Lives of Priests.* New York: Seminar Press, 1973. 291pp.

This is the report on the behavioral science diagnosis of the Catholic Archdiocese of Hartford. There were three major purposes of the study: to present a theory of career development in organizations which draws on a number of social and behavioral science disciplines and which work under clearly and uniquely defined organizational conditions: Catholic diocesan priests; and to study intensively the careers of priests as a distinctive group of working men. The study indirectly addresses some issues about leadership experiences and skills.

HOCKING, David L. *Be a Leader People Follow.* Ventura, CA: Regal Books, 1979. 192pp.

The author has been pastor of Grace Brethren Church in Long Beach since 1968. He teaches bible on a radio broadcast. This book contains his seven principles for good leadership: example, communication, ability, motivation, authority, strategy and love.

JACKSON, B. F., Jr., ed. *Communication-Learning for Churchmen.* Nashville: Abingdon, 1968. 303pp.

This four part, four author book addresses the principles and practice of communications and learning. It describes the process from a theological perspective. It treats how to use print and audiovisual resources in the communication process.

JOHNSON, Luke T. *Decision Making in the Church: A Biblical Model.* Philadelphia: Fortress Press, 1983. 109pp.

There should be a close connection between what a group claims to be and the way it does things. This is the basic premise of the author, associate professor of religious studies at Indiana University. He examines the nature of decision making and the many New Testament texts which treat decisions. He leads the reader to the understanding that a community of faith needs to make decisions in correspondence with the theology it believes in. Finally, he suggests a model for a truly pastoral and theological way of making decisions true to scripture, tradition and experience.

JUDY, Marvin T. *The Multiple Staff Ministry.* Nashville: Abingdon, 1969. 287pp.

This book is the result of extensive research and accumulation of data from 1400 churches representing 22 denominations. This work contains theoretical material (theology, sociology, etc.), analytical material (statistics) and practical material (administrative procedures). After introductory chapters on leadership, personnel management and group dynamics, the author treats each position found in churches with multiple staffs.

KNUDSEN, Raymond B. *Models for Ministry: Creative Administration in the Local Church.* New York: Friendship Press, 1978. 98pp.

The author, a United Presbyterian pastor, is the director of the National Consultation on Financial Development. This book, one of several in church leadership, collects his experiences and ideas on church management. It treats such topics as interpersonal communication skills, program development, use of facilities and space, scheduling, finances and goal setting.

LEAS, Speed B. *Discover Your Conflict Management Style.* Washington: Alban Institute, 1984. 23+pp.

This is an instrument to help people become aware of appropriate conflict strategies and their own preferred styles. This booklet contains the questions, the score sheet and the interpretation of the scores.

LEAS, Speed B. *Leadership and Conflict.* Nashville: Abingdon, 1982. 124pp.

The book is addressed to all leaders in organizations, not just to those who are formally elected or appointed. All leaders will find themselves in conflict situations. Dr. Leas, the director of consulting with the Alban Institute, teaches how to handle conflict competently. He starts by developing a theory of human needs and then focuses on the theory of leadership and the effect of fear on conflict dynamics. He also discusses uncovering suppressed conflict, dealing with organizations as systems, curing conflict, as well as, creating conflict.

LEAS, Speed B. and Paul Kittlaus. *Church Fights: Managing Conflict in the Local Church.* Philadelphia: Westminster Press, 1973. 186pp.

This book is written for pastors and lay persons who are interested in applying the behavioral sciences to their churches. It provides concepts, experiences, processes and tools for congregational leaders desiring to lead a congregation through conflict in such a way that the conflict is useful to the further development of the mission of the church. The appendices give material on where and how professional consultants can be found, on win/lose behavior in competing groups, on the use of simulation games for developing conflict management skills and a design for training referees.

LePEAU, Andrew T. *Paths of Leadership.* Downers Grove, Il: InterVarsity Press, 1983. 126pp.

The author believes that each person must be a leader in some way or another. Leadership is a function or process that moves from person to person in a group. He writes about the character of leaders not about what a leader does. Christian growth takes place in an environment of serving, following, facilitating, teaching, modeling and envisioning. The author explains each of these paths of leadership.

LEWIS, G. Douglass. *Resolving Church Conflicts: A Case Study Approach For Local Congregations.* New York: Harper and Row, 1981. 182pp.

The purpose of this book is to aid individuals and institutions in becoming more effective managers of conflict. It is based on the belief that all of us have or can develop the capacity to experience and use conflict so that it becomes a stimulation to our growth and development. The author designed the volume so that it moves from theory toward practice. There is a series of cases which serve as the link from theory to practice.

LYONS, Bernard. *Leaders for Parish Councils: A Handbook of Training Techiques.* Techny, IL: Divine Word Publications, 1971. 151+pp.

A parish council in the Catholic Church is the group of lay members who represent the full membership and collaborate with the pastor for the growth of the parish. This book describes the nature and function of this council. It suggests guidelines for the selection of council membership. Finally it maps out a training program for council leadership.

McDONOUGH, Reginald M. *Keys to Effective Motivation.* Nashville: Broadman, 1979. 140pp.

Relying on the works of Maslow and Shostrom, the author discusses the themes of motivation and manipulation. After exposing the shortcomings of manipulation, he offers four keys to effective motivation: stabillity, teamwork, affirmation and challenge.

McSWAIN, Larry L. and William C. Treadwell, Jr. *Conflict Ministry in the Church.* Nashville: Broadman, 1981. 202pp.

This book was written to help analyze the conflicts, disagreements, and tensions which arise in all churches. It is a practical guide for dealing with conflict. The authors' thesis is that conflict situations offer the christian an opportunity to minister to others as a reconciling servant of Jesus Christ. Both authors are associated with the Baptist Church.

MILLER, John M. *The Contentious Community: Constructive Conflict in the Church.* Philadelphia: Westminster Press, 1978. 107pp.

The author has served as pastor of a Presbyterian Church for several years. He reflects on his experiences of tensions among church individuals and groups. He believes that the normal polarities which create tension can be used to strengthen the church congregation. Each chapter treats a different aspect of tension and conflict. There is a series of discussion questions at the end of the book.

O'BRIEN, J. Stephen, ed. *Gathering God's People: Signs of a Successful Parish.* Washington, DC: National Catholic Education Association, 1982. 265pp.

This is a collection of short essays on the American Catholic parish. It was designed as a study resource in harmony with the NCCB's statement THE PARISH, A PEOPLE, A MISSION, A STRUCTURE. Each chapter concludes with a summary and suggested readings. It is intended as an educational tool for parish groups.

OLSEN, Frank H. *Church Staff Support: Cultivating and Maintaining Staff Relationships.* Minneapolis: Augsburg, 1982. 39pp.

Pastors and lay professionals need support. They need someone to lean on and share their concerns with. This book describes the need for this support and offers a model for establishing a staff support group. It outlines the purposes and objectives of such a group and lists the benefits which will be derived.

RASSIEUR, Charles L. *Stress Management for Ministers.* Philadelphia: Westminister Press, 1982. 168pp.

As a Presbyterian pastor and psychotherapist, the author has assisted innumerable pastors in their quest for good health. This book aims at helping clergy manage their stress particularly by taking responsibility for themselves as persons. The work contains verbatim observations of pastors. The main chapters discuss the ten areas of the pastor's life and ministry which prove to be most stressful.

REDIGER, Lloyd G. *Coping with Clergy Burnout.* Valley Forge, PA: Judson Press, 1982. 110pp.

Clergy are in a stressful vocation. This book shares the author's insights which he gained from many years as a counselor through the Office of Pastoral Services for the Wisconsin Conference of Churches. After describing burnout, the author explains the prescription to prevent it: AIM. This stands for awareness, input and management.

RUSBULDT, Richard E. *Basic Leader Skills: Handbook for Church Leaders.* Valley Forge: Judson Press, 1981. 63pp.

The handbook for lay leadership is divided into five chapters: who is a leader, styles of leadership, functions of a leader, effective church planning and managing conflict. Each chapter explains the theory and gives exercises for the group to do. The last ten pages are a guide for those who would be leading the training sessions.

RUSBULDT, Richard E., Richard K. Gladden and Norman M. Green, Jr. *Local Church Planning Manual.* Valley Forge, PA: Judson, 1977. 248pp.

This manual is designed to assist a congregation in its planning. It is written as a practical tool. With definitions, illustrations and steps, it will lead a planning group from writing the purpose statement to goal setting, mission design, mission management and finally, evaluation. The authors have included also 150 pages of appendixes.

RUSH, Myron D. *Management: A Biblical Approach.* Wheaton, IL: Victor, 1983. 236pp.

This book is designed to provide the principles of management outlined in the bible. It also supplies the leadership and management tools needed to apply these biblical principles of management successfully. The author is the owner of a manufacturing firm and a consultant for business firms and christian organizations. He attemps to write for the christian businessman as well as the church leader. There is a chapter on team spirit, planning, decision-making, communication skills, delegation, time management, conflict, and the christian manager's role in society.

SHAWCHUCK, Norman. *How To Manage Conflict in the Church.* Indianapolis: Spiritual Growth Resources, 1983. 51pp.

This title is published in two volumes, Vol. 1: UNDERSTANDING AND MANAGING CONFLICT; Vol. 2: CONFLICT INTERVENTIONS AND RESOURCES. The first volume addresses the theory of conflict and assesses conflict management styles. It is written in a workbook form. The second volume gives readings on the topic and other resources.

SWEETSER, Thomas P. *The Catholic Parish.* Chicago: Center for the Scientific Study of Religion, 1974. 134pp.

This book deals with shifting membership patterns in the American Catholic parish since Vatican II. The purpose of this volume is to provide information based on a group of Catholic parishes which can be used as a comparison for other parish situations. Eight suburban communities with ten parishes were studied. There is a chapter on each of the following topics: the response of the clergy, the reaction of the laity, the function and role of a Catholic parish and finally, the reasons for changing membership.

TIDWELL, Charles A. *Working Together through the Church Council.* Nashville: Convention Press, 1968. 114pp.

The church council of the Southern Baptist Convention is an advisory body which is involved in planning, coordinating and evaluating church programs and services. The author, an associate professor of church administration, explains every aspect of this council: how to form one, how to conduct a council meeting, how the council plans, coordinates and evaluates church programs. This book is written for use in a study group.

WOOD, James R. *Leadership in Voluntary Organizations.* New Brunswick, N.J.: Rutgers University Press, 1981. 140pp.

This is a critique of Robert Michels' POLITICAL PARTIES (1962). The author demonstrates, using data collected from churches, that leaders who control the organization do not necessarily displace the group's goals. This book focuses on how formal legitimacy and belief in legitimacy facilitate transcendence. The thesis of the author is that policies out of line with members' desires may result from the attempts of leaders to carry out their responsibility to direct the group in the implementation of its values.

ZACCARIA, Joseph S. *Facing Change.* Minneapolis: Augsburg, 1984.

The author is a professor of educational psychology at the University of Illinois and an active church member. In the first part of this book, he describes the nature of change and the pressure that change creates for the local congregation. Change presents the church with a challenge. The second part of the book highlights one of a number of problem-solving methods. The author has adapted the method of Morris and Shashkin (ORGANIZATION BEHAVIOR IN ACTION, 1976) to form his own spiritual/secular problem-solving method.

ZEHRING, John William. *Working Smart: A Handbook for New Managers.* Garrett Park, MD: Garrett Park Press, 1985. 78pp.

It is not enough to work hard, one must work smart. The author, vice-president of Bangor Theological Seminary, explains how to be a manager and survive not only in business but in ministry. He treats communication skills, computer skills, and methods of motivation. (from a review by Manfred Holck, Jr.).

CHAPTER SIX

Leadership and Management

ADAMS, Arthur Merrihew. *Effective Leadership for Today's Church.* Philadelphia: Westminster Press, 1978. 190pp.

The author is an experienced Presbyterian pastor and professor at Princeton Theological Seminary. He intends this book for pastors and church officers. After two chapters on the spiritual role of the pastors, the following chapters treat the topics of authority, leadership styles, organizations, communications, planning and staff relationships.

ADAMS, Arthur Merrihew. *Pastoral Administration.* Philadelphia: Westminster Press, 1964. 174pp.

The author intends this work to be of practical help to pastors and those preparing for the ministry. The first section explains the principles of administration and its practice in the church. The second section discusses the traditional parish programs from the point of view of leadership. The last chapter is on success and failure. The author is a Presbyterian pastor and professor of church administration.

ADAMS, Jay E. *Shepherding God's Flock.* Grand Rapids: Baker Book House, 1979. 530pp.

This is three books in one volume. The first section on pastoral life treats the practical questions about the ministry such as making house calls, visiting the sick, managing time, etc. The second section is on pastoral counseling. The third section is on pastoral leadership. In it the author discusses his views of authority, delegation, communication, planning, program design, finance and other administrative topics.

ANDERSON, James D. *To Come Alive!* San Francisco: Harper & Row, 1973. 141pp.

The author, a church planner, shares what he has learned about member motivation, sources of power, utilization of conflict, leadership and management of change. A blend of theology and behavioral science theory, this book is filled with examples and case studies. It offers practical suggestions to reorganize congregational structures.

ANDERSON, James D. and Dale G. Lake. *From Information to Action: Information Systems and the Use of Knowledge.* Washington: Alban Institute, 1974. 48pp.

This is a monograph from a reseach project the authors did for the Episcopal Diocese of Washington D.C. It lays the groundwork for a comprehensive understanding of the role of information on the processes of institutional change. The paper also discusses the different kinds of information needed at various stages of creative problem-solving. While the context of the paper is a specific question for a particular church, the theory is universally applicable.

ANDERSON, James D. and Ezra Jones. *The Management of Ministry.* San Francisco: Harper and Row, 1978. 202pp.

The book proposes to help local church ministers understand their role and to manage their ministry more effectively. The authors contend that church management is too narrow a focus. They prefer to address the management of ministry because ministry is a system of relationships which interact with each other.

ANDERSON, Ray S. *Minding God's Business.* Grand Rapids: Wm. Eerdmans Publishing Co, 1986. 156pp.

The author is professor of theology and ministry at Fuller Theological Seminary and a lecturer in the Institute for Christian Organizational Development there. He presents a biblical and theological basis for understanding the unique characteristics of christian organizations and what it means to manage them in a christian way. He discusses the role of leadership in managing christian organizations and addresses such issues as strategic planning, mission statements and ethical questions facing the leader.

ARN, Win, ed. *The Pastor's Church Growth Handbook.* Pasadena: Church Growth Press, 1979. 223pp.

This volume collects a number of articles published over the years in CHURCH GROWTH: AMERICA. They all fall under the general rubric of "How to improve and enlarge your church." There are chapters on training laity, building morale, advertising and reaching ethnics.

ASHEIM, Ivar and Victor R. Gold, eds. *Episcopacy in the Lutheran Church: Studies in the Development and Definition of the Office of Church Leadership.* Philadelphia: Fortress Press, 1970. 261pp.

This is a historical and theological study of the development and meaning of the office of leader in the Lutheran Church. By tracing historical lines and transitions over time and cultures, it attempts to give the younger churches of Asia and Africa some assistance in answering the questions about what must be held constant and what can be adapted to local conditions.

BARRS, Jerram. *Shepherds and Sheep: A Biblical View of Leading and Following.* Downers Grove, IL: InterVarsity Press, 1983. 98pp.

This is a biblical critique of common leadership patterns which the author has identified in various church groups. By recalling the New Testament doctrine of the priesthood of believers, Christians will avoid current abuses of shepherding and eldership, especially the trend toward leadership to assume more authority than God intends.

BEHRING, Mark C. *A Strategy for Growth at Zion Lutheran Church Through Pastoral Leadership and Leadership Development.* Unpublished D.Min. Dissertation: Fuller Theological Seminary, 1985. 196+pp.

This is a study of pastoral leadership and its application to Zion Lutheran, whose pastor is the author. After a theological treatise on ministry, leadership and growth, this Doctor of Ministry dissertation treats pastoral leadership from the point of view of the pastor, the staff and lay leadership. The annual leadership retreat and a working plan for intentional leadership concludes the work.

BERGHOEF, Gerard and Lester Dekoster. *The Elders Handbook: A Practical Guide for Church Leaders.* Grand Rapids: Christian's Library Press, 1979. 303pp.

The authors, laymen with experience in Christian Churches, have structured this practical handbook on the teaching of Acts 20:28-31. There are chapters on leadership, management, preaching, worship, marriage, counselling and instruction, youth work, and visiting the sick. It is written for leaders of all Protestant communions.

BEVERIDGE, Wilbert E. *Managing the Church.* Naperville, IL: SCM Book Club, 1971. 124pp.

The author, a member of the department of Management Studies at Middlesex Polytechnic, writes from his British experience and point of view. He discusses the nature and structure of groups and various organizations using the findings of behavioral science. He applies this knowledge to the church. He concentrates on how "management by objectives" can be used effectively in parishes and specialized ministries (e.g. industrial chaplaincies).

BLACKWOOD, Andrew Watterson. *Pastoral Leadership.* Nashville: Abingdon, 1949. 272pp.

The author intends this work to be a textbook on church management. He borrowed heavily from business management. In the first part he treats the pastor as executive (forming a team with others) and in the second part he deals with the pastor as organizer (setting the stage for someone else to work). Each chapter ends with a list of suggested readings.

BORMANN, Ernest and Nancy Bormann. *Effective Committees and Groups in the Church.* Minneapolis: Augsburg, 1973. 104pp.

This is a practical book about groups in the church. The authors apply communication theory to the experience of various kinds of committees and groups. The work is divided into three areas: group dynamics, leadership and small group communication.

BOYAJIAN, Jane A., ed. *Ethical Issues in the Practice of Ministry.* Minneapolis: United Theological Seminary of the Twin Cities, 1984. 98pp.

This volume presents a rich ecumenical discussion of ethical issues in the work of ministry. Most of the authors first presented their ideas at the conference "Ethics and the Practice of Ministry" held in Minneapolis in 1981. After introductory chapters on philosophy and method, the book contains reflections on the ethics of preaching, social ministry, counselling and interim ministry.

BRODERICK, Robert C. *Your Parish Where the Action Is.* Chicago: Franciscan Herald Press, 1974. 50pp.

This book addresses the training of lay leaders in the Catholic parish. The author explains the nature of leadership, suggests elements of a training program and outlines the committees which will lead to effective action.

BROWN, Cecil Dene. *The Effect of Leadership Style on Selected Variables of Church Growth.* Unpublished Ed.D. dissertation: University of Oklahoma, 1984. 121 l.

Using a survey of ministers and other records, the author measured the correlation between the pastor's leadership styles and church's administative styles in regard to their effect on membership attendance and budget. He found that when the styles were both democratic or both autocratic, there was no effect on the variables. When there was a conflict of styles, there was a change in the variables. The study was carried out in the Oklahoma United Methodist Conference.

BUTT, Howard. *The Velvet Covered Brick.* New York: Harper and Row, 1973. 186pp.

The subtitle of this book is: Christian Leadership in an Age of Rebellion. The author takes a fresh look at authority and submission from the christian point of view. He describes the christian leader in new terms and explains the revolution which brews in the ranks of organizations.

BUTTON, Lewis I. *A Self-Description with Analysis of the Management Styles of Independent, Fundamental Pastors.* Eastern Baptist Theological Seminary: Unpublished D.Min. dissertation, 1983. 196pp.

As the title explains, this dissertation for the Doctor of Ministry at Eastern Baptist Theological Seminary reports the findings from a survey of pastors associated with the Independent Fundamental Churches of America. The leadership styles of these pastors are compared and contrasted with the study of leadership in the bible. There is also a short review of literature in church management.

CALIAN, Samuel Carnegie. *Today's Pastor in Tomorrow's World.* New York: Hawthorn, 1977. 153pp.

Building on the research of the Association of Theological Schools' Readiness for Ministry Project, the author identifies eight current models of ministry. After some evaluation of each, he proposes his model: the pastor as grass-roots theologian. He gives the scriptural and theological foundation for this model and applies it to several aspects of pastoral ministry.

CAMPBELL, Thomas C. and Gary B. Reierson. *The Gift of Administration*. Philadelphia: Westminster Press, 1981. 139pp.

Why do ministers have to be administrators? Because administration is a spiritual gift through which ministry happens. This is the thesis of this little book which started as a series of lectures by Campbell and was completed by Reierson. It is a scriptural and theological study of the administrative tasks of stewards, elders, bishops and deacons.

CARNAHAN, Roy E. *Creative Pastoral Management*. Kansas City, MO: Beacon Hill Press, 1976. 119pp.

The author is an administrator of the church of the Nazarene after serving as a pastor for many years. In this book he has written about the main elements of church leadership and management from his experience. He concludes the work with a chapter on evaluation and a number of appendices containing sample budgets and forms.

CLAGETT, John Y. *Management for the Self-Governing Church*. Buffalo Grove, IL: J.Y. Clagett, 1983. 151pp.

Leaders in self-governing churches who are not confident with their role desciptions will find much practical advice in this book. It covers such topics as planning, budgeting, managing time, decision-making, motivation and training other leaders.

COLEMAN, William V., ed. *Parish Leadership Today*. West Mystic, CT: Twenty-Third Publications, 1979. 93pp.

This selection of writings from TODAY'S PARISH magazine focuses on the imperative of effective leadership. There are articles on the parish and its leaders, the parish council, the role of pastor and current issues in the Catholic parish church.

DALE, Robert D. *Ministers as Leaders*. Nashville: Broadman Press, 1984. 132pp.

This book explains leadership styles. It offers some theological reflections on various styles and gives examples on how to match leader and follower styles. The last section illustrates the interactive leadership style. The author is a professor of pastoral leadership and church ministries at Southeastern Baptist Seminary.

DALE, Robert D. *Pastoral Leadership.* Nashville: Abingdon Press, 1986. 240pp.

The author presents his ideas on the basis of pastoral leadership in a congregational setting. He describes pastoral leadership and gives some theological, biblical and philosophical bases for its understanding. He discusses leadership styles and the skills needed in a leader. The last chapters deal with personal issues facing a church leader.

De THOMASIS, Louis. *My Father's Business: Creating a New Future for the People of God.* Westminster, MD: Christian Classics, 1984. 167pp.

Convinced that the church can benefit from the insights of business management, the author argues that a major obstacle to introducing these insights is the strong resistance to any type of management in the ministry. The book presents and summarizes many of the major classical and contemporary contributions to the art and science of management. It will serve as a primer for those engaged in church administration. (From a review by Kevin Sullivan).

DEEGAN, Arthur X. *The Priest As Manager.* New York: The Bruce Publishing Co, 1969. 154pp.

For this author the manager is the coordinator of the activities of others. The functions of a manager are planning, organizing, directing, motivating and controlling. This book aims to help the priest be more effective as an administrative leader. It discusses the process of management and the development of management theory. It explains the use of time, the art of delegation, styles of leadership, management by objectives and problem solving. The author concludes the book with a case study.

DIETTERICH, Paul and Russell Wilson. *A Process of Local Church Vitalization.* Naperville: Center for Parish Development, 1976. 328pp.

This is the fourth report in Experiment in District Revitalization of the United Methodist Church. After extensive research, the report presents a model of church renewal. Chapter six treats the training and development of leaders for the future.

DITZEN, Lowell Russell. *Handbook of Church Administration.* New York: MacMillan, 1962. 390pp.

This volume summarizes the author's many years as a pastor and administrator in the Presbyterian Church. He has outlined the main tasks and functions of a church leader and collected information which clearly shows that a pastor is also a manager of a "business". The book emphasizes the central role of lay people in administration.

DOOHAN, Helen. *Leadership in Paul.* Wilmington, DE: Michael Glazier, 1984. 208pp.

Starting with the premise that understanding the scriptures is necessary for understanding christian leadership, this study of Pauline writing examines leadership in the early church. The author, assistant professor of Religious Studies at Gonzaga University, presents the social and religious environment of each Pauline letter and shows the style of leadership used to solve conflicts and direct the development of the christian communities.

DOUTY, Mary Alice. *How To Work with Church Groups.* Nashville: Abingdon Press, 1957. 170pp.

This book attempts to put principles of group work and of democratic group leadership into practical terms. It is written for the church group leader or teacher. There are chapters on evaluating groups, group patterns, group organization, understandings, procedure, and techniques for good group functioning. There are chapters treating the specific concerns of groups in the church-school program.

DUDLEY, Carl S. *Making the Small Church Effective.* Nashville: Abingdon, 1978. 192pp.

This book tells the story of the small and effective congregation. From years of study and giving workshops the author analyzes the strengths of the small church and explains the dynamics that have been proven successful. He offers helpful resources, practical exercises and tested tools to those charged with the leadership of these congregations.

EIMS, LeRoy. *Be the Leader You Were Meant To Be: What the Bible Says About Leadership.* Wheaton, IL: Victor Books, 1975. 132pp.

The author is director of evangelism for the Navigators. The book is an outgrowth of his personal study of the Scriptures and his work in training christian leaders. Each chapter presents a quality or characteristic of a christian leader as found in the bible, especially in the lives of biblical figures.

ELLIS, Joe S. *The Church on Purpose: Keys to Effective Church Leadership.* Cincinnati: Standard Publishing Co, 1978. 222pp.

Written with the hope that it would be used as a textbook for christian leaders, this volume presents a philosophy of the church as a foundation for ministry leadership and administration. It deals with the purpose of the church, conditions essential to achieving that purpose, factors that tend to obscure or displace that purpose and solutions to these problems.

ENGSTROM, Ted W. and Edward R. Dayton. *The Art of Management For Christian Leaders.* Waco, TX: Word Books, 1976. 285+pp.

This book contains both theory and practice. It treats the question of the nature of christian leadership and how it differs from secular organizations. The authors, well known for their publications, write about planning, leadership skills, hiring staff and managing time, meetings and interruptions.

ENGSTROM, Ted W. and Edward R. Dayton. *The Christian Executive.* Waco, TX: Word Books, 1979. 216pp.

These well-known authors collaborate again for this, their fourth book. They continue to address the practical and daily issues of the church leader. They first focus on the job and skills of the manager/minister. Then the focus shifts to the people a minister gathers around him. Finally the book treats of the church organization itself.

ENGSTROM, Ted W. and Edward R. Dayton. *The Christian Leader's 60-Second Management Guide.* Waco, TX: Word Books, 1984. 143pp.

These experienced and prolific authors have put the principles and practice of successful church management into thirty short chapters. The issues, questions and conflicts common to christian leaders are discussed here.

ENGSTROM, Ted W. *The Making of a Christian Leader*. Grand Rapids, MI: Zondervan, 1976.

This book was written according to the author "to help the christian leader get a clearer picture of what he wants to do and be in a church or organization." After three chapters exploring the scriptural teaching, the author explains the styles of leadership, the price of leadership and how to develop leadership skills. The final chapters treat motivation, planning and taking control.

ENGSTROM, Ted W. *Your Gift of Administration: How to Discover and Use It*. Nashville, TN: Thomas Nelson, 1983. 172pp.

The author contends that there are two gifts of administration: official and charismatic. He wrote this book to help official leaders develop and strengthen their administrative gifts and to help charismatic leaders be more effective in their administrative responsibilities. He first addresses the personal gifts of a church administrator. Then he analyzes administration as a function or office. In the final section the author explains how to put the charismatic and official sides of administration together.

FICHTER, Joseph H. *Organization Man in the Church*. Cambridge, MA: Schenkman, 1974. 167pp.

The author, a sociologist of religion, has collected his talks which treat of the sociology of organized American religion as exemplified mainly by the Catholic Church. The unifying theme is that religion is a major institution in our American socio-cultural system. The talks are grouped into three categories: church personnel, church structure and the relationship of the church to broader aspects of the social world.

FLUCKIGER, W. Lynn. *Dynamic Leadership*. Salt Lake City: Deseret Book Co, 1962. 113pp.

This book is divided into four sections. The first gives reasons why the pursuit of excellence in leadership is a desirable goal. The second section deals with the traits of character and personality of a successful leader. Section Three spells out leadership techniques. The last section contains inspirational thoughts on citizenship.

FORD, George L. *Manual on Management for Christian Workers.* Grand Rapids: Zondervan, 1964. 152pp.

The author served sixteen years as a pastor and ten years as Executive Director of the National Association of Evangelicals. He writes from his experience and insight. This is a general treatment of the major themes of church management with strong influence from biblical literature. It is aimed at all christians who manage, but especially church administrators.

GANGEL, Kenneth O. *Competent to Lead.* Chicago: Moody Press, 1974. 144pp.

The purpose of this volume is to speak specifically to the issue of human relations in the church and its affiliate organizations. This is done by drawing principles from both similar research and biblical texts, in an effort to blend the two into a Christian philosophy of collective service and ministry. The audience is lay persons of the evangelical church who need to understand and practice professional administration.

GARDINER, M. James. *Program Evaluation in Church Organization.* Winter Park, FL: Anna Publications Inc., 1977. 128pp.

The author, a Presbyterian minister and consultant in church organization, has written this for the day to day managers of the church's activities. He discusses in clear language the basic principles of program evaluation and explains, in practical terms, the evaluation process. In the appendix he offers a sample evaluation report (summer work camps for minority youth).

GLASSE, James D. *Putting it Together in the Parish.* Nashville: Abingdon, 1972. 159pp.

"The present-day pastor has at his disposal a remarkable range of resources. If he can put all this together in the parish he can have a creative and effective ministry. This book is a report of some professional models and strategies that I have observed while watching responsible pastors at work around the country. The emphasis is on getting started, simple disciplines that set the direction for the pastor in his professional development... The disciplines I propose are designed to enable the pastor to 'factor out the variables,' then 'put it all together' in fresh and fruitful ways." (From the author's preface).

GRAY, Rhea, et al. *Experiences in Activating Congregations: A Cross Denominational Study*. Chicago: Institute for Ministry Development, 1978. 114pp.

This is a report of an action-research project to study theory and practice for revitalizating churches. It is intended to be helpful to church leaders, judicatory officials, national program agency staff and consultants. This study brought together a psychological tradition which emphasized voluntary behavioral change and achievement motivation and a wholistic organizational approach to congregations which emphasized the contributions of classical organizational theory as well as more contemporary theories and methods (including Etzioni's theory of activation). The church communities studied were Roman Catholic, Lutheran and Presbyterian. (from the Preface.).

GREELEY, Andrew et al. *Parish, Priest and People: New Leadership for the Local Church*. Chicago: Thomas More Press, 1981. 262pp.

This is an interdisciplinary study of pastoral leadership in the local church. This collaboration between social scientists and theologians reflects on various aspects of the local religious community (church). The second part examines the leadership of the local church, emphasizing the priestly function. The third section treats the issue of educating the religious leader especially in the skills of preaching.

GREENLEAF, Robert K. *The Servant as Religious Leader*. Peterborough, NH: Center for Applied Studies, 1982. 56pp.

This monograph is the latest in a series written by this author. The purpose of this work is to increase the number of capable and motivated religious leaders. The first sections are dedicated to describing the leader and examining some examples. There is a section on teaching leadership in seminaries. The last sections deal with pitfalls and new frontiers.

HAGGAI, John E. *Lead On!* Waco: Word Books, 1986. 208pp.

The author, founder of the Haggai Institute for Advanced Leadership Training in Singapore, has taught the content of this book to leaders of the Third World. He has summed up true leadership in twelve principles. Each principle forms a chapter of the book. While the principles are intended to apply universally, they come out of a distinct christian context and experience.

HALL, Brian and Helen Thompson. *Leadership through Values.* New York: Paulist Press, 1980. 111pp.

In his preface, Hall describes the genesis of this book and the unique contribution of Thompson. Thompson wrote the text under the supervision of Hall who had developed the theory. In the first chapter the main theories of leadership are briefly explained. In the second chapter Hall's theory on the development of consciousness and values is set forth. The next chapter describes seven leader-follower styles and addresses the process by which a person goes through them. The final chapter examines the motivation of leaders.

HALL, Brian P. *Shepherds and Lovers.* Ramey, N.J: Paulist Press, 1982. 75pp.

This is a guide to spiritual (healthy) leadership and christian ministry. The author begins with a chapter on leadership and ministry and explains how they should be linked in the christian. The rest of the book explores this idea and demonstrates methods to accomplish it.

HALL, Douglas T. and Benjamin Schneider. *Organizational Climates and Careers: The Work Lives of Priests.* New York: Seminar Press, 1973. 291pp.

This is the report on the behavioral science diagnosis of the Catholic Archdiocese of Hartford. There were three major purposes of the study: to present a theory of career development in organizations which draws on a number of social and behavioral science disciplines and which work under clearly and uniquely defined organizational conditions: Catholic diocesan priests; and to study intensively the careers of priests as a distinctive group of working men. The study indirectly addresses some issues about leadership experiences and skills.

HENDRIX, Olan. *Management for the Christian Worker.* Santa Barbara, CA: Quill Publications, 1976. 130pp.

Having conducted management skill workshops for 15 years in 28 countries, the author has finished this text for leaders of church organizations. It is a thorough, practical guide to effective church management. After describing the problem and identifying responsibilites, the book treats planning, goal setting, running groups, delegation and decision-making.

HILLOCK, Wilfred M. *Involved: An Introduction to Church Participation and Management.* Nashville: Southern Publishing Association, 1977. 155pp.

The author is a professor of business and economics. He has lectured widely in management training programs. From his experience in the christian church, he believes that good church management will result in good participation by lay people. This book is aimed at those who are responsible for church activities. It will offer them the principles for good management. There are chapters on principles, goal setting, authority, choosing leaders, evaluation, problem solving and church growth.

HOCKING, David L. *Be a Leader People Follow.* Ventura, CA: Regal Books, 1979. 192pp.

The author has been pastor of Grace Brethren Church in Long Beach since 1968. He teaches bible on a radio broadcast. This book contains his seven principles for good leadership: example, communication, ability, motivation, authority, strategy and love.

HOLCK, Manfred, Jr. *Clergy Desk Book.* Nashville: Abingdon, 1985. 288pp.

This is a book for parish pastors. It treats the major topics of church administration: ministers as managers and leaders, organizing the church, staff, volunteers, programming, property and plant, communications, salary, bookkeeping, fund-raising, computers, membership recruitment and taxes. It is meant to be a practical help so sample forms and charts are included. It has a small bibliography and helpful index.

HOWSE, W. L. *The Church Staff and Its Work.* Nashville: Broadman, 1959. 174pp.

The author, a member of the Southern Baptist Church, explains the role of each key staff person in a church. His focus is the educational ministry. He addresses the leadership qualifications of staff members and methods of developing leadership.

HOWSE, W. L. and W. O. Thomason. *A Church Organized and Functioning.* Nashville: Convention Press, 1963. 148pp.

This work is the result of information gathered from twenty- one Baptist churches regarding their function. The book is organized as a text for classroom use. It is intended for those who wish more knowledge about the organization of the church and its leadership roles.

HUBER, Evelyn M. *Enlist, Train, Support Church Leaders*. Valley Forge, PA: Judson Press, 1975. 32pp.

The author is Program Associate in Leader Development in the American Baptist churches. This is a practical book aimed at assisting a church in the task of assessing the need for leaders, securing the right persons and offering them support in their new roles.

HULME, William E. *Managing Stress in Ministry*. New York: Harper and Row, 1985. 145pp.

Unlike other books on the same subject this one assumes that the clergy have distinct resources for the handling of stress in their own religious tradition. The author, a Lutheran seminary professor, believes that the ministry itself is a stress reducer. After introductory chapters on the nature and relation of stress to the clergy, the book treats the religious resources for coping such as faith, grace and prayer. The final chapters treat practical steps which can be taken to reduce stress.

HULME, William E. *Your Pastor's Problems*. Minneapolis: Augsburg, 1967. 165pp.

The pastor's problems with people, the church organizations and with himself are explored in this book. The ten chapters cover such topics as the need to succeed, the pastor's family, loneliness, use of time and living a balanced life.

HUTCHESON, Richard G., Jr. *Wheel Within the Wheel: Confronting the Management Crisis of the Pluralistic Church*. Atlanta: John Knox Press, 1979. 238pp.

This is a scholarly treatise on church management. It begins with an historical look at the church's organizational heritage. The current management theories and techniques are then examined. Finally, practical applications for the local congregations are presented. This section deals with leadership issues, managerial models, evaluation, goal-setting, and organizational restructuring. The author served as a Navy chaplain and wrote his doctoral dissertation on this subject.

JOHNSON, Luke T. *Decision Making in the Church: A Biblical Model.*
Philadelphia: Fortress Press, 1983. 109pp.

There should be a close connection between what a group claims
to be and the way it does things. This is the basic premise of the
author, associate professor of religious studies at Indiana
University. He examines the nature of decision making and the
many New Testament texts which treat decisions. He leads the
reader to the understanding that a community of faith needs to
make decisions in correspondence with the theology it believes in.
Finally, he suggests a model for a truly pastoral and theological
way of making decisions true to scripture, tradition and
experience.

JONES, Ezra Earl. *Strategies for New Churches.* New York: Harper and
Row, 1976. 178pp.

"How do you go about organizing a new church in your
community?" This book addresses the many facets of this
question. The author first provides a historical, theological and
sociological overview of the nature and function of the local
church. He continues with the actual process of organizing new
congregations. He analyzes the needs of various types of
churches: suburban, special purpose, downtown and others. The
author has been the associate director of research for the United
Methodist Board of Global Ministries.

JUDY, Marvin. *The Cooperative Parish in Nonmetropolitan Areas.*
Nashville: Abingdon, 1967. 208pp.

The author presents his research on various forms of cooperative
parishes in rural America. He examines the nature of
nonmetropolitan society and parish structures. He then discusses
the cooperative parish itself and its leadership. The final chapter
presents the basis of his research.

JUDY, Marvin T. *The Multiple Staff Ministry.* Nashville: Abingdon,
1969. 287pp.

This book is the result of extensive research and accumulation of
data from 1400 churches representing 22 denominations. This
work contains theoretical material (theology, sociology, etc.),
analytical material (statistics) and practical material
(administrative procedures). After introductory chapters on
leadership, personnel management and group dynamics, the
author treats each position found in churches with multiple staffs.

KATZ, Irving I. and Myron E. Schoen. *Successful Synagogue Administration.* New York: Union of American Hebrew Congregations, 1963. 200pp.

This is a manual of administration for the synagogue leader. It is addressed to rabbis, cantors, educators as well as professional administrators and lay committeepersons. It treats such issues as the board of trustees, committee structure, finances, maintenance, membership and the synagogue office.

KEATING, Charles J. *The Leadership Book.* New York: Paulist Press, 1978. 133pp.

This volume relates the insights of the behavioral sciences to the fields of religion and spirituality. It examines theories of management and shows their practical application in areas of church leadership. Topics include a theology of leadership, the dimensions of leadership, ways of handling conflict, the use of feedback, and structures for decision making. The author is a consultant and educator. He served as Director of Religious Education and Continuing Education for the Catholic diocese of Camden.

KEATING, Charles J. *Pastoral Planning Book.* New York: Paulist Press, 1981. 73pp.

Planning is an art. The more we master it, the easier it becomes. The author has written this practical book to assist readers to develop this art. He begins with reflections on leadership style and the traits of followership. These influence planning. He then discusses ways to determine needs. The process of planning is considered next. The meaning of God's revelation and God's plan is reflected on. The final chapter speaks of community research. The work contains diagrams and work sheets useful for a parish setting.

KILINSKI, Kenneth K. and Jerry C. Wofford. *Organization and Leadership in the Local Church*. Grand Rapids: Zondervan, 1973. 253pp.

The book is based upon three assumptions. There is a change in our society which is fundamental and involves the disappearance of traditional values; there are certain principles of church dogma which are essential to survival and effectivness of the church; and there are certain freedoms of the church which are not restrained by the scripture and within which the church can operate to fulfil its basic purposes. The purpose of this book is to examine the local church in the midst of the forces generated by our age and to analyze the primary functions of the church in light of the challenges before us. Part one considers the challenge of guiding christians toward spiritual maturity. Part two considers the role and functions of the church leader for equipping others to do the work of ministry. Part three examines the administration and organization of the church.

KIRK, Richard J. *On the Calling and Care of Pastors*. Washington, D.C: Alban Institute, 1973. 12pp.

"The purpose of this paper is to sketch out some ways of improving the working relationship between a pastor and a congregation in such a way that the clergyperson feels a greater sense of fulfillment and satisfaction in his or her work and the parish feels that the ministry which it needs and desires is being carried out effectively." (p. 2).

KNUDSEN, Raymond B. *Models for Ministry: Creative Administration in the Local Church*. New York: Friendship Press, 1978. 98pp.

The author, a United Presbyterian pastor, is the director of the National Consultation on Financial Development. This book, one of several in church leadership, collects his experiences and ideas on church management. It treats such topics as interpersonal communication skills, program development, use of facilities and space, scheduling, finances and goal setting.

KNUDSEN, Raymond B. *New Models for Church Administration: The Practical Application of Business Principles*. Chicago: Association Press, 1979. 165pp.

The third in a series of new models books. The author applies them to the administration of the local church. After introducing the book with a chapter comparing the common elements of business and religion, he treats long-range planning, funding, budgeting, stewardship, staffing and leadership.

LAMBERT, Norman M. *Managing Church Groups.* Dayton, OH: Pflaum, 1975. 85pp.

The author has developed a system of church management which fits into the overall field of organizational development. He calls this system Church Management by Objectives and Results. It balances the task with the process. It can be used by individuals or groups. This book is a manual for this system. It is written in a practical, learning style.

LARSON, Philip M., Jr. *Vital Church Management.* Atlanta: John Knox Press, 1977. 120pp.

This book addresses the problem of good management in parishes. The author uses the image of "health" when he speaks of "coming alive", "life and death", "adding new blood" etc. These are part of the titles of chapters on business principles, membership recruitment, building programs, fund-raising, counseling etc. There is also a chapter on building a new church.

LEACH, William H. *Handbook of Church Management.* Englewood Cliffs, NJ: Prentice-Hall, 1958. 503pp.

This is a classic textbook on church management. It applies the science of management to religious organizations. The first part addresses the usual topics. The last part speaks of areas more commonly referred to today as ministry. This treatment would be judged today as too organizational.

LEAS, Speed B. *Leadership and Conflict.* Nashville: Abingdon, 1982. 124pp.

The book is addressed to all leaders in organizations, not just to those who are formally elected or appointed. All leaders will find themselves in conflict situations. Dr. Leas, the director of consulting with the Alban Institute, teaches how to handle conflict competently. He starts by developing a theory of human needs and then focuses on the theory of leadership and the effect of fear on conflict dynamics. He also discusses uncovering suppressed conflict, dealing with organizations as systems, curing conflict, as well as, creating conflict.

LEAS, Speed B. *"Should The Pastor Be Fired?"*: *How to Deal Constructively With Clergy-Lay Conflict.* Washington: Alban Institute, 1980. 22pp.

This monograph reports the findings and learnings from 128 situations in which clergy were "fired". The causes, the methods, the pains and some resolutions are explained. The purpose of this work is to assist all involved to approach the question of clergy termination with more understanding and skill.

LePEAU, Andrew T. *Paths of Leadership.* Downers Grove, Il: InterVarsity Press, 1983. 126pp.

The author believes that each person must be a leader in some way or another. Leadership is a function or process that moves from person to person in a group. He writes about the character of leaders not about what a leader does. Christian growth takes place in an environment of serving, following, facilitating, teaching, modeling and envisioning. The author explains each of these paths of leadership.

LINDGREN, Alvin J. *Foundations for Purposeful Church Administration.* New York: Abingdon, 1965. 302pp.

"This is not a book about church administration but a guiding statement for church administrations. The focus is upon preparing the minister to be a church administrator by interpreting what church administration is, the foundations on which it rests, and the prerequisites for leadership in this field.... It will be strongly emphasized throughout (the book) that at the basic foundation on which all church administration rests is a clear understanding of the christian faith and of the mission of the church." (From the author's introduction) The author taught for many years at Garrett Theological Seminary.

LINDGREN, Alvin and Norman Shawchuck. *Management for Your Church.* Nashville: Abingdon, 1977. 156pp.

This is a book on the theory and practice of managing a church organization. Church management is viewed within the total context of the practice of ministry and a systems theory is applied to it. This systems perspective is built on the foundations and principles of church administration found in Lindgren's FOUNDATIONS FOR PURPOSEFUL CHURCH ADMINISTRATION.

LLOYD, Kent and Kendall Price. *The Church Executive: Building the Kingdom through Leadership Development.* Inglewood, CA: Public Executive Development and Research, 1967. 90pp.

The authors describe the experience and explore the implications of the 1966 seminar on executive leadership sponsored by the Church of the Latter Day Saints. The seminar attempted to apply the science of organizational management to the executive positions of the church.

LUECKE, David S. and Samuel Southard. *Integrating Ministry and Management in the Church.* Waco: Word Books, 1986. 207pp.

Administration is one of the most disliked of pastoral responsibilities. The authors of this book grapple with pastoral administration and by placing the emphasis on the word "pastoral" create a new framework and rationale for becoming an effective administrator. Although written for evangelical Protestant ministers, there is something here for everyone.

LUECKE, David S. and Samuel Southard. *Pastoral Administration.* Waco: Word Books, 1986. 207pp.

The subtitle of this volume is: Integrating Ministry and Management in the Church. The authors have chosen six areas of pastoral experience. One begins the chapter with a case study and proceeds to pull out the principles and pastoral practice at work. The other author concludes the chapter with his comments and reflections. The areas treated are management issues in a pastoral setting.

LYONS, Bernard. *Leaders for Parish Councils: A Handbook of Training Techiques.* Techny, IL: Divine Word Publications, 1971. 151+pp.

A parish council in the Catholic Church is the group of lay members who represent the full membership and collaborate with the pastor for the growth of the parish. This book describes the nature and function of this council. It suggests guidelines for the selection of council membership. Finally it maps out a training program for council leadership.

MacNAIN, Donald T. *The Growing Local Church.* Grand Rapids: Baker Book House, 1975.

The author, a Presbyterian minister, has divided this work into four parts. The first part is a biblical reflection on the church as an organization. The second part deals with both the office and work of the pastor-teacher. The third part treats the office and work of various church officials. The final part discusses the decision making and leadership role of the congregation.

MAVIS, W. Curry. *Advancing . . . the Smaller Church.* Grand Rapids: Baker Book House, 1968. 180pp.

The author writes about the urban and rural church with fewer than 150 members. He discusses principles which underlie effective work in these churches. He treats such topics as planning, organizing, budgeting, public relations, worship and education.

McCARTT, Clara Anniss. *How to Organize Your Church Office.* Westwood, NJ: Fleming H. Revell Co, 1962. 63pp.

The author was an instructor in Church Office Procedures at Southern Baptist Theological Seminary. She writes this practical book to assist pastors in being more efficient with their time and energy. The book considers the common concern of church office space, material and equipment.

McKENZIE, Leon. *Decision Making in Your Parish: How to Consult the Local Church.* West Mystic, CT: Twenty-third Publications, 1980. 152pp.

This book is about the mechanics of conducting most surveys in parishes and local churches. It discusses designing the instrument, sample size, random selection, cover letters, nonresponse and interpretation of data. There are three appendices with further practical helps.

MEAD, Daniel L. and Darrel J. Allen. *Ministry by Objectives.* Wheaton, IL: Evangelical Teacher Training Association, 1978. 79pp.

These ministers have applied MBO principles to the ministry. This book blends the motivating "whys" with the realistic "how to" methods. Practical management activities--"practivities"--have been integrated in the content with the goal of producing more effective workers for God.

MEAD, Loren B. *The Developmental Tasks of the Congregation in Search of a Pastor.* Washington, D.C: Alban Institute, 1977. 8pp.

The author describes five developmental tasks which a congregation should address while it searches and selects a new pastor. The concept of a developmental task is borrowed from Erickson.

NEWSOME, Robert R. *The Ministering Parish: Methods and Procedures for the Pastoral Organization.* New York: Paulist Press, 1982. 101pp.

This book is the result of grass-roots work done by the Parish Corporate Renewal Network in Chicago and the Pastoral Alliance for Corporate Renewal in Toledo. The four facets of parish renewal which are treated in this volume are: vision, staff development, structures and ministry. The intent of this work is not simply to educate the laity but to establish a mutual grouping in a deep sense of communion out of which life and service together flow. The author is a clinical psychologist specializing in organizational development and human resources training.

O'BRIEN, Gary Donald. *Developing a Collegial Style of Leadership: Sharing Responsibility in the Local Religious Community.* Unpublished D.Min. dissertation: The Catholic University of America, 1984. 203pp.

In this Catholic University Doctor of Ministry dissertation, the author studies the principles and dynamics of a collegial style of leadership. Using the research of Rensis Likert, the author actually conducted a project of developing and implementing a collegial model of leadership in a religious community retreat house. The heart of the project was a three-day workshop on this style of leadership. This dissertation reports on the method and results of the project.

OSWALD, Roy M. *New Beginnings.* Washington, D.C: Alban Institute, 1977. 80pp.

This is a work book for ministers beginning a new pastorate. Its format combines explanations of topics and written exercises. The topics cover termination, making entry and analyzing the new responsibility.

OSWALD, Roy M. *The Pastor As Newcomer.* Washington, D.C: Alban Institute, 1977. 12pp.

This monograph reports the results of a study of turnover of clergy and professional church workers. In 1976 the Alban Institute assisted the American Lutheran Church to learn more about transitions in their system and how to effectively support and help those affected by this turnover.

OSWALD, Roy M. *Power Analysis of a Congregation.* Washington, DC: Alban Institute, 1981. 15pp.

The author wants to help church leaders understand power and authority better, come to grips with their theology of power, and become comfortable using the power and authority available to them. In this monograph, he analyzes various kinds of personal power and corporate power, and shows how clergy and laity exercise authority through their roles in their congregations.

OSWALD, Roy M. *Running through the Thistles.* Washington, D.C: Alban Institute, 1978. 20pp.

This monograph is subtitled: Terminating a Ministerial Relationship within a Parish. It is an essay based on the author's experience and data collected through a study conducted by the Alban Institute. The author presents some suggestions for making termination a more positive experience.

PENDORF, James G. and Helmer C. Lundquist. *Church Organization: A Manual for Effective Local Church Administration.* Wilton, CT: Morehouse-Barlow, 1977. 125pp.

The authors, widely experienced in leadership of the Episcopal Church, have written this manual for all levels of church leadership. After a chapter on the history of the organization of the Episcopal Church, they describe the principles of church management and each position in particular. The appendix carries a complete suggested job description for each office.

PIERSON, Robert H. *How To Become a Successful Christian Leader.* Mountain View, CA: Pacific Press Publishing Association, 1978. 172pp.

This is literally a "how-to" book. Each of the fifteen chapter titles begins with "How to ...." The author, an elder in the Seventh Day Adventist Church, writes a series of practical hints about how to get more work done, how to set goals and how to be a spiritual leader. His main sources for this work are his experience, the scriptures and church documents.

PIERSON, Robert H. *So You Want To Be a Leader! A Spiritual, Human Relations and Promotional Approach to Church Leadership and Administration.* Mountain View, CA: Pacific Press Publishing Association, 1966. 152pp.

The author writes from his personal experience as an Adventist pastor and administrator, especially in Southern Asia. He has subtitled the book: A Spiritual, Human Relations, and Promotional Approach to Church Leadership and Administration. The emphasis has been placed on the spiritual aspects (scripture) and common sense approaches to administration.

PORCHER, Philip. *What You Can Expect from an Interim Pastor.* Washington, D.C: Alban Institute, 1980. 8pp.

This small monograph discusses what a congregation can expect from an interim pastor and an interim consultant. There are both pros and cons for this temporary arrangement.

POWERS, Betty and Jane E. Mall. *Church Office Handbook for Ministers.* Valley Forge, PA: Judson Press, 1983. 80pp.

The pastor is responsible for the administration of the church office. This book aims to help pastors understand the mission and purpose of the office so he or she can get others to help do the work more efficiently. The book treats the various functions of the church office in a practical way, often with sample forms and useful hints.

POWERS, Bruce P. *Christian Leadership.* Nashville: Broadman Press, 1979. 133pp.

The author has written this book on the premise that christian leadership is not so much a goal to be achieved as it is a means or a life-style that must be developed. He explains the various functions of leadership: relating to others, implementing change, working with groups and believing in God.

POWERS, Bruce P., ed. *Church Administration Handbook*. Nashville: Broadman Press, 1985. 318pp.

This book is designed as a general reference for both ministers and ministerial students. The content moves sequentially through three broad categories: how a minister relates to organizations and to people (chapters 1-3); how a minister performs administrative functions (chapters 4-5); and how a minister relates to self and colleagues (chapters 6-8). Each chapter provides basic information, then gives guidelines and procedures related to the topic. There is a bibliography at the end of each chapter for further information. (from the preface).

RICHARDSON, Lovella Stoll. *Handbook for the Church Office*. Cincinnati: Standard Publishing, 1972. 151pp.

This handbook will help the church worker understand and accomplish administrative duties associated with the ministry. It is a reference work for the church office. It treats such practical topics as hiring the church secretary, office equipment, files, letters, and keeping records.

RUDGE, Peter F. *Management in the Church*. London: McGraw Hill, 1976. 172pp.

In the first section of this book the author establishes the relevance of management in the church. A case is made in each of the various fields of management (personnel, financial, property, household, office, time) and the case is argued on a very practical level. The second section describes new intiatives for restructuring the church, using examples from the Catholic Church. It is then demonstrated that this new church idiom bears close resemblance to management concepts found in the business world.

RUETER, Alvin C. *Personnel Management in the Church*. Minneapolis: Augsburg Publishing House, 1984. 56pp.

The author contends that every church has an operative personnel policy. Too many of these policies are implicit and informal. He attempts to explain how to formulate an intentional personnel policy through the use of examples and stories. The Lutheran Church provides the majority of examples. The author treats the personnel committee, employment practices, position descriptions, performance evaluation and fair compensation.

RUSBULDT, Richard E. *Basic Leader Skills: Handbook for Church Leaders.* Valley Forge: Judson Press, 1981. 63pp.

The handbook for lay leadership is divided into five chapters: who is a leader, styles of leadership, functions of a leader, effective church planning and managing conflict. Each chapter explains the theory and gives exercises for the group to do. The last ten pages are a guide for those who would be leading the training sessions.

RUSH, Myron D. *Management: A Biblical Approach.* Wheaton, IL: Victor, 1983. 236pp.

This book is designed to provide the principles of management outlined in the bible. It also supplies the leadership and management tools needed to apply these biblical principles of management successfully. The author is the owner of a manufacturing firm and a consultant for business firms and christian organizations. He attemps to write for the christian businessman as well as the church leader. There is a chapter on team spirit, planning, decision-making, communication skills, delegation, time management, conflict, and the christian manager's role in society.

SAFRANSKI, Scott R. *Managing God's Organization: The Catholic Church in Society.* Ann Arbor., MI: UMI Research Press, 1985. 199pp.

This volume is the revision of the author's doctoral dissertation. It studies the Catholic Church from an organizational, not theological perspective. The focus is the interaction of units, at various levels of the church's hierarchy, with groups outside the church. Church organization and management processes are then studied in terms of adaptations made in an effort to assume cooperation and stable relationships with important internal and external interest groups and resource suppliers. The work contains the results of an empirical case study in which the resource dependence model was applied to one archdiocese.

SCHALLER, Lyle E. and Charles A. Tidwell. *Creative Church Administration*. Nashville: Abingdon, 1975. 208pp.

This book attempts to address the issue of church management from the point of view of creativity. The first chapter discusses the values which influence the creativity of the leader. This initial chapter is devoted to suggesting how the organizational structure can be altered to increase participation, enthusiasm, creativity, and openness to innovation. The second chapter presents different planning models. The remaining chapters are on motivation, volunteers, listening, recruitment, salaries, and evaluation.

SCHALLER, Lyle E. *Activating the Passive Church: Diagnosis and Treatment*. Nashville: Abingdon, 1981. 159pp.

After identifying a dozen systems for classifying churches, the author elaborates on one system: internal dynamics. The passive congregation is described both in its causes and in its effects. Alternatives to the passive church are suggested. The author concludes the book with ideas about making a smooth transition from one pastor to another and how new members can be used in establishing an effective church program.

SCHALLER, Lyle E. *Assimilating New Members*. Nashville: Abingdon, 1978. 128pp.

This book focuses on the outreach of existing congregations to people who are not actively involved in the life of any worshiping congregation. It is directed to the leaders, both clergy and lay, who are concerned about reaching and assimilating new members into the congregation. The approach of the author is to assist the reader to examine experiences and basic assumptions. There are chapters on why people are discouraged from membership and chapters on how to include new members.

SCHALLER, Lyle E. *The Change Agent*. Nashville: Abingdon, 1972. 207pp.

The basic thesis of this book is that a systematic and anticipatory approach to planned social change is the most effective style for an agent of change. The author discusses the nature of change, offers models for a process of change, describes the agent of change, discusses power and explains the anticipatory style of leadership.

SCHALLER, Lyle E. *Getting Things Done: Concepts and Skills for Leaders*. Nashville: Abingdon, 1986. 144pp.

The author assumes that leadership skills can be taught. He writes this book for those who want to learn how to lead and how to organize for action, two sides of the same coin. There are chapters on organization, leadership, styles of leadership and groups which get things done.

SCHALLER, Lyle E. *Looking in the Mirror: Self-Appraisal in the Local Church*. Nashville: Abingdon, 1984. 206pp.

The central goal of this book is to help congregational leaders expand their conceptual framework and ask new questions in self-appraisal efforts. The first four chapters raise broad general questions about the distinctive nature of the worshiping congregations. The next seven chapters focus on various aspects of congregational life ranging from the turning points of the past to the characteristics of today's members to the conceptual framework for program planning. The last three chapters raise questions that frequently are overlooked about youth ministries, nursery schools and the building planning committee.

SCHALLER, Lyle E. *The Middle Sized Church: Problems and Prescriptions*. Nashville: Abindgon, 1985. 160pp.

This book is directed to leaders of churches averaging between 100 and 200 at worship. After describing the middle sized church and its distinctive character, the author then writes about the six dominant personalities of its members. The next topic is the low self-esteem of leaders of this church. Finally the financial picture of the middle sized church is presented.

SCHALLER, Lyle E. *The Multiple Staff and the Larger Church*. Nashville: Abingdon, 1980. 142pp.

While the number of large (800-1,000 members) churches is relatively small (5-7% of each denomination) they are different from the smaller congregations. This book addresses those differences. There are chapters on the staffing question, the senior minister and the associate minister.

SCHALLER, Lyle E. *The Pastor and the People,* rev. ed. Nashville: Abingdon, 1986.

This revised edition of the 1973 book addresses the experience of choosing a new pastor. It looks at this issue from the point of view of the congregation, the search committee and the pastor. There are chapters on the process of identifying the needs of the church and the strengths of a pastor, the compensation package, the pastor's first year and evaluating the total effectiveness of the church.

SCHALLER, Lyle E. *The Small Church IS Different.* Nashville: Abingdon, 1982. 191pp.

This work treats the church which averages fewer than 40 members at worship. The author believes that the majority of the churches in this country are this size. His premise is that these churches are radically different from larger congregations. This book describes the small church, discusses areas of congregational life in which size is a very significant factor, answers many questions about how these churches keep going and looks at the future.

SCHALLER, Lyle E. *Survival Tactics in the Parish.* Nashville: Abingdon, 1977. 208pp.

The author envisions this book as a sequel to his 1973 THE PASTOR AND THE PEOPLE. This volume follows the same mythical Don Johnson as he completes a nine-year pastorate at St. John's Church. The first three chapters are intended to be a part of an education program as the pastor reflects on his career. The next two chapters are directed at a broader congregational audience and discusses the "signs" surrounding every church and the invisible reward system. The following six chapters are intended to stimulate congregational thinking about such issues as lay leadership, community image and goal setting. The final four chapters focus on the role of the pastor, this time from a joint congregational-ministerial perspective.

SCHOEN, V. W. *God's Need.* Washington, DC: Review and Herald Publishing Assoc, 1976. 176pp.

The author lays down ten principles of christian leadership. While intended for the lay people of the Seventh-day Adventist churches, they also apply to all christian denominations.

SEIFERT, Harvey and Howard J. Clinebell, Jr. *Personal Growth and Social Change: A Guide for Ministers and Laymen as Change Agents.* Philadelphia: Westminster Press, 1969. 240pp.

This book views pastors as agents of change. As counselors, teachers and managers, they will be more effective if they understand the dynamics and skills of change. The authors treat this topic theoretically and practically.

SHAWCHUCK, Norman. *Taking a Look at Your Leadership Styles.* Downers Grove, IL: Organization Resources Press, 1977. 47pp.

This is a workbook on leadershp styles. It begins with an inventory survey. After the reader has scored the survey, the workbook guides the reader through the explanation of the styles. It also contains readings on various leadership cases.

SLAGHT, Lawrence T. *A Single Board for Churches.* Valley Forge, PA: Judson Press, 1979. 169pp.

This little volume addresses the question of how to set up a single board for more effective and efficient administration of a local church. After arguing for a single board, the author describes its function and the eight committees it might have. There are several appendices. The first describes how one church changed from a multiple to a single board.

SMITH, Fred. *Learning To Lead: Bringing Out the Best in People.* Carol Stream, IL: Word Books, 1986. 182pp.

This is the fifth volume in a new series by the editors of LEADERSHIP magazine. After many years in the business world, the author writes about how the minister can develop as a leader. Besides some theoretical considerations there are practical methods and stories about others who have succeeded. (from an advertisment).

SMITH, Rockwell, ed. *Sociological Studies of an Occupation: The Ministry*. Roswell, NM: Hall-Poorbaugh Press, 1979. 68pp.

Four areas of ministry practices researched by extensive use of questionnaires. The areas are: the ministry of the laity, women in ministry, conflicting perspectives on the minister's role and supervision of the minister. The study was conducted by the Leiffer Bureau of Social Religious Research on the Illinois United Methodist Church.

STATON, Knofel. *God's Plan for Church Leadership*. Cincinnati: Standard Publishing, 1982. 155pp.

The author studies the biblical principles and corresponding practices that he judges are essential for effective christian leadership. The leadership of Jesus is explained. There are chapters on Paul, Barnabas, the apostles, the pastors, and the elders. The final chapters analyze the biblical findings.

STONE, Sam E. *The Christian Minister*. Cincinnati: Standard Publishing, 1980. 252pp.

The author examines the role of the minister in the bible and in the present church. He studies the minister's personal life, his relationships and his job. In the last section, the topics include preaching, counseling, administration and conducting services. Each chapter contains questions to think about, a list of additional resources, and project ideas.

STRANG, Stephen E., ed. *Solving the Ministry's Toughest Problems, Vol I*. Altamonte Springs, Fl: Strang Communications Co, 1984. 430pp.

There are sixty articles which have appeared in MINISTRIES: THE MAGAZINE FOR CHRISTIAN LEADERS. The articles have been categorized under such headings as solving administration problems, solving pastoral problems, solving education problems, solving building problems, etc.

SUGDEN, Howard F. and Warren W. Wiersbe. *Confident Pastoral Leadership.* Chicago: Moody Press, 1973. 160pp.

The authors have had many years of pastoral experience in the Baptist Church. They have collected the most frequently asked questions about pastoral leadership. This book answers those questions. The questions are grouped in chapters treating the call to ministry, the pastor of a new church, church organization, preaching, the pastor's books, visitation, marriage and divorce, death and funerals, church discipline, the pastor and his home and the pastor's priorities.

SWINDOLL, Charles. *Leadership: Influence That Inspires.* Waco: Word Books, 1985. 72pp.

This small volume is a treatise on leadership from the biblical point of view. The author has searched the scriptures for the essence of leadership and the characteristics of both effective and ineffective leadership. The teaching of the bible is applied to the practical tasks of church leadership today.

SWINDOLL, Charles R. *Hand Me Another Brick.* Nashville: Thomas Nelson, 1978. 207pp.

This is a biblical treatise on leadership. Each chapter explores the scripture for examples of the theme being treated, e.g., training for leadership, motivation, discouragement, etc. These ideas were first given as sermons and lectures at leadership seminars.

Theology, News and Notes-Alumni Newsletter. Pasadena, CA: Fuller Theological Seminary, 1973. 23pp.

This little booklet reprints seven articles on the topic of management in the church which appeared in earlier newsletters. The authors are experienced and recognized experts. They explain their ideas in goal setting, priorities, planning and motivation.

TIDWELL, Charles A. *Working Together through the Church Council.*
Nashville: Convention Press, 1968. 114pp.

The church council of the Southern Baptist Convention is an
advisory body which is involved in planning, coordinating and
evaluating church programs and services. The author, an
associate professor of church administration, explains every
aspect of this council: how to form one, how to conduct a council
meeting, how the council plans, coordinates and evaluates church
programs. This book is written for use in a study group.

United Church of Christ. *The Ministry of Volunteers.* United Church of
Christ, Office for Church Life and Leadership, 1979.

This is a series of several booklets on the topic of volunteers in
church ministry. The titles of each booklet are: 1. Volunteers and
Volunteer Ministries; 2. The Church and Its Volunteers;
3. Guiding the Church's Volunteer Ministry Program; 4.
Developing a Mission Statement; 5. Training Volunteers; 6.
Supporting Volunteers; 7. Completing Volunteer Ministries. The
series describes and resources a program for recruiting and
developing volunteer ministries.

United Methodist Church. *Guidelines for Leadership in the Local Church.*
Nashville: Abingdon, 1984.

This is a series of thirty booklets which provide guidance for
leaders of local churches. The booklets treat such topics as
administrative boards, role of the pastor, finances, mission and
each ministry of the church. The booklet describes the topic and
how it is to be organized. These guidelines were prepared by the
Interagency Task Force on Resources of the United Methodist
Church.

VASSEL, Bruno. *Lengthen Your Leadership Stride.* Bountiful, Utah:
Horizon Publishers, 1983. 142pp.

This book treats the training and development of lay leaders in the
Church of Jesus Christ of Latter-day Saints. It blends good
business practices with insights and experiences the author has
gained from his numerous leadership responsibilities.

WAGNER, C. Peter. *Leading Your Church Growth*. Ventura, CA: Regal Books, 1984. 224pp.

This is a book about leadership for church membership growth. The author explores the question: Why does a strong leadership influence positive growth? He addresses the leader as enabler, the art of followership, calling the right pastor and planning effective outreach.

WALRATH, Douglas A. *Leading Churches Through Change*. Nashville: Abingdon, 1979. 124pp.

This is a collection of six case studies of churches and change. In each case the author explains the problem, the solution and applications to other situations. The author is a church development consultant who formerly served as an executive with the Reformed Church in America.

WALRATH, Douglas A. *Planning for Your Church*. Philadelphia: Westminster Press, 1984. 112pp.

This work describes ways and means of effective long-range planning within a congregation. The author uses a team approach and emphasizes basic planning which sets overall goals and fashions programs to accomplish the goals. After focusing on the minister's own style of leadership and the choice of the planning committee, he looks at the process of community analysis. He then shows how to establish priorities and achieve consensus for a plan of action. The author is professor of Pastoral Studies at Bangor Theological Seminary.

WHEELEY, B. Otto and T. Cable. *Church Planning and Management*. Philadelphia: Dorrance and Co, 1975. 218pp.

The authors, industrial executives and members of Baptist congregations, write about the basic principles of management applied to all protestant churches. The volume is a handbook for local congregations. The chapters on planning, organization, constitutions, finances, education, recreation, worship and promotional methods are general, practical and accompanied by charts.

WHITE, Ray L. *How To Get Things Done.* Salt Lake City: Bookcraft, 1968. 164pp.

The author, a leader in the Church of Jesus Christ of Latter-day Saints, writes about the theory and practice of leadership for the believer. He covers planning, decision-making, and delegation. He gives practical hints on how to run a meeting and how to involve more people in the life of the church. It is aimed at the church membership who are all leaders.

WHITE. Robert N., ed. *Managing Today's Church.* Valley Forge: Judson, 1981. 192pp.

This book comes out of five years of church management seminars held at the Babcock Graduate School of Management of Wake Forest University. The authors are seminar faculty members. They write about the fundamentals of management in a church environment. There is a chapter on the role and duties of the pastor. Planning is treated in three chapters (strategic, short-term and annual financial planning). After the chapter on marketing, three chapters follow on human resource management. The final chapter is on time management.

WICK, Calhoun W. *The Management Side of Ministry.* Toledo: Wick Press, 1976. 89pp.

This is a typewritten manuscript. It is intended to be a practical help to church leaders. It gives step by step suggestions toward solving problems. The author treats such topics as: the mission of a church, managing the church year, problem-solving, and other practical issues which involve church management.

WILLIAMS, Denny. *Leadership Life-Style.* Kansas City, MO: Beacon Hill Press, 1983. 120pp.

The author, an ordained minister and a doctor of business administration, explains the basic principles of staff management. He directs his writing to the pastor and others who have positions of leadership in the local church. This volume is divided into six main headings. Each heading contains many topics which cover, on average, two pages. Every aspect of parish administration, organization, personnel service, advertising and office management is treated in practical fashion.

WILLIAMS, George M. *Improving Parish Management.* Mystic, CN: Twenty-Third Publications, 1983. 98pp.

The author, a retired businessman, writes about the fundamentals of managing a parish from the Catholic experience. He treats such topics as planning, organizing, training, delegating, managing volunteers, scheduling and running effective meetings.

WOOD, James R. *Leadership in Voluntary Organizations.* New Brunswick, N.J.: Rutgers University Press, 1981. 140pp.

This is a critique of Robert Michels' POLITICAL PARTIES (1962). The author demonstrates, using data collected from churches, that leaders who control the organization do not necessarily displace the group's goals. This book focuses on how formal legitimacy and belief in legitimacy facilitate transcendence. The thesis of the author is that policies out of line with members' desires may result from the attempts of leaders to carry out their responsibility to direct the group in the implementation of its values.

YEAGER, William E. *Who's Holding the Umbrella?* Nashville: Thomas Nelson, 1984. 204pp.

The author has served as pastor of a Baptist church. He writes about leadership by way of examples and incidents which happened to him or to his colleagues. He develops the image which appears in the title: the church leader is the one who holds the umbrella over the congregation to protect it from forces which could hurt and destroy.

ZEHRING, John William. *Working Smart: A Handbook for New Managers.* Garrett Park, MD: Garrett Park Press, 1985. 78pp.

It is not enough to work hard, one must work smart. The author, vice-president of Bangor Theological Seminary, explains how to be a manager and survive not only in business but in ministry. He treats communication skills, computer skills, and methods of motivation. (from a review by Manfred Holck, Jr.).

CHAPTER SEVEN

Planning

ADAMS, Arthur Merrihew. *Effective Leadership for Today's Church.* Philadelphia: Westminster Press, 1978. 190pp.

The author is an experienced Presbyterian pastor and professor at Princeton Theological Seminary. He intends this book for pastors and church officers. After two chapters on the spiritual role of the pastors, the following chapters treat the topics of authority, leadership styles, organizations, communications, planning and staff relationships.

ADAMS, Jay E. *Shepherding God's Flock.* Grand Rapids: Baker Book House, 1979. 530pp.

This is three books in one volume. The first section on pastoral life treats the practical questions about the ministry such as making house calls, visiting the sick, managing time, etc. The second section is on pastoral counseling. The third section is on pastoral leadership. In it the author discusses his views of authority, delegation, communication, planning, program design, finance and other administrative topics.

ALLRED Thurman W. *Basic Small Church Administration.* Nashville: Convention Press, 1981. 64pp.

This is a practical "how-to" book aimed at pastors of small, rural churches having Southern Baptist affiliation. The authors are mostly experienced pastors who discuss skills such as administration, programming, decision-making, planning and budgeting.

ANDERSON, Ray S. *Minding God's Business.* Grand Rapids: Wm. Eerdmans Publishing Co, 1986. 156pp.

The author is professor of theology and ministry at Fuller Theological Seminary and a lecturer in the Institute for Christian Organizational Development there. He presents a biblical and theological basis for understanding the unique characteristics of christian organizations and what it means to manage them in a christian way. He discusses the role of leadership in managing christian organizations and addresses such issues as strategic planning, mission statements and ethical questions facing the leader.

BROHOLM, Richard R. *Strategic Planning for Church Organizations.* Valley Forge, PA: Judson, 1969. 32pp.

This booklet clearly outlines a process of strategic planning which could easily be used in church organizations. The last chapter adapts the process to personal planning. The author includes a glossary of terms.

BROWN, J. Truman. *Church Planning a Year at a Time.* Nashville: Convention Press, 1984. 24pp.

This booklet is a practical guide to church planning. It contains very little theory. There are numerous charts, timelines and questions which a planning group could use in its work.

CALLAHAN, Kennon L. *Twelve Keys to an Effective Church: Strategic Planning for Mission.* San Francisco: Harper and Row, 1983. 127pp.

This is a detailed explanation of strategic long-range planning for the local church. The keys mentioned in the title are the factors which are characteristic of successful missionary churches. Half are relational and half are functional characteristics. The author is a planning consultant with 23 years of experience. He writes in a clear, straightforward style.

CLAGETT, John Y. *Management for the Self-Governing Church.* Buffalo Grove, IL: J.Y. Clagett, 1983. 151pp.

Leaders in self-governing churches who are not confident with their role desciptions will find much practical advice in this book. It covers such topics as planning, budgeting, managing time, decision-making, motivation and training other leaders.

CONLAN, Douglas R. and J. Douglas Varey. *Planning for More Effective Ministry.* Ontario, Canada: Distribution Services, 1974. 62pp.

This short, photocopied work is a very practical guide for church planning. It is designed to be used step by step without any explanation of theories or principles.

DAVIS, Warren B. and Richard M. Cromie. *The Future is Now: A Beginning Guide for Long-Range Planning in Your Church.* Pittsburgh: Desert Ministries, 1984. 94+pp.

The authors intend this little book to be a how-to manual. It is the result of their working together as pastor and lay leader in a Presbyterian church in Pennsylvania. They collected the guidelines for long range planning which they successfully used. They explain how they began with techniques from the corporate world and adapted them to church congregations.

DEEGAN, Arthur X. *The Priest As Manager.* New York: The Bruce Publishing Co, 1969. 154pp.

For this author the manager is the coordinator of the activities of others. The functions of a manager are planning, organizing, directing, motivating and controlling. This book aims to help the priest be more effective as an administrative leader. It discusses the process of management and the development of management theory. It explains the use of time, the art of delegation, styles of leadership, management by objectives and problem solving. The author concludes the book with a case study.

DIETTERICH, Paul M. *A Practical Guide to Church Planning.* Chicago: The Center for Parish Development, 1981. 342pp.

The Center for Parish Development has many resources for planning. The Center's executive director has gathered them in this practical guide. Besides the standard planning steps, this 3-ring binder book, begins with a chapter on building a planning team.

ENGSTROM, Ted W. and Edward R. Dayton. *The Art of Management for Christian Leaders.* Waco, TX: Word Books, 1976. 285+pp.

This book contains both theory and practice. It treats the question of the nature of christian leadership and how it differs from secular organizations. The authors, well known for their publications, write about planning, leadership skills, hiring staff and managing time, meetings and interruptions.

ENGSTROM, Ted W. *The Making of a Christian Leader.* Grand Rapids, MI: Zondervan, 1976.

This book was written according to the author "to help the christian leader get a clearer picture of what he wants to do and be in a church or organization." After three chapters exploring the scriptural teaching, the author explains the styles of leadership, the price of leadership and how to develop leadership skills. The final chapters treat motivation, planning and taking control.

FLYNN, Leslie B. *How to Save Time in the Ministry.* Nashville: Broadman Press, 1966. 95pp.

"Work smarter not harder" is the motto of this practical booklet on efficiency. The author has gathered experiences and suggestions from pastors and other religious leaders. The chapters discuss such topics as delegation, planning ahead, scheduling, using spare minutes, starting earlier and taking time off.

HENDRIX, Olan. *Management for the Christian Worker.* Santa Barbara, CA: Quill Publications, 1976. 130pp.

Having conducted management skill workshops for 15 years in 28 countries, the author has finished this text for leaders of church organizations. It is a thorough, practical guide to effective church management. After describing the problem and identifying responsibilites, the book treats planning, goal setting, running groups, delegation and decision-making.

HEYD, Thomas. *Planning for Stewardship.* Minneapolis: Augsburg, 1980. 40pp.

This is a practical book about developing a giving program for church congregations; after explaining the biblical meaning of stewardship, the author treats planning and organizing a stewardship program. There are five pages of exhibits.

HINTON, Leonard C. *Census Data Manual for Church Planning: To Be Used by Churches in Cities (places) of 50,000 or More Population or in Any Tracted Area.* Atlanta: Southern Baptist Convention, Home Mission Board, 1982. 76pp.

This manual is designed for church planners who wish to use 1980 census data to assist them in knowing more about their community or "church field"... The manual emphasizes selected church-related data and suggests ways it can be used in church planning... One of the difficulties in using census data is that there is so much information that a person who is unfamiliar with it can easily become bewildered and frustrated. This work singles out 19 key items called indicators which can be used to make generalizations about the population for a given area under consideration. (From the Introduction).

HOFFMAN, Douglas R., ed. *The Energy-Efficient Church: How to Save Energy (and Money) in Your Church.* New York: Pilgrim Press, 1979. 85pp.

This practical, detailed book was prepared by Total Environment Action, Inc. of Harrisville, New Hampshire. It was written for the office of Architecture of the United Methodist Church. It treats the principles of energy conservation and how to make the right decisions. Several chapters explain the details of building and energy conservation methods.

HUDNUT, Robert K. *Arousing the Sleeping Giant: How to Organize Your Church for Action.* New York: Harper and Row, 1973. 186pp.

The author has applied the ideas and suggestions found in this book to St Luke Presbyterian Church in Minneapolis. He has written from the conviction that planning will make the church count for something. The book basically addresses the various aspects of planning for the local church. Several introductory chapters discuss the theological and biblical basis for planning.

JOHNSON, Douglas W. *The Care and Feeding of Volunteers.* Nashville: Abingdon, 1978. 125pp.

This volume offers a realistic and effective approach to the development and maintenance of church volunteers. The author's basic assumption is that a volunteer is a human being with real needs. He writes about the role of volunteers, identifying and recruiting volunteers, giving them assigments, planning with volunteers, running meetings and training volunteers. Dr Johnson is executive director of the Institute for Church Development.

KEATING, Charles J. *Pastoral Planning Book.* New York: Paulist Press, 1981. 73pp.

Planning is an art. The more we master it, the easier it becomes. The author has written this practical book to assist readers to develop this art. He begins with reflections on leadership style and the traits of followership. These influence planning. He then discusses ways to determine needs. The process of planning is considered next. The meaning of God's revelation and God's plan is reflected on. The final chapter speaks of community research. The work contains diagrams and work sheets useful for a parish setting.

KILLACKEY, Edward R. *Pastoral Planning: A Process for Discernment.* Kampala, Uganda: Gaba Publications, 1975. 77pp.

This is one of a series of papers published by the Pastoral Institute of Eastern Africa. The author is a Marykroll priest who has extensive experience in leading planning workshops. This paper is the result of these experiences. It is a tactical manual for pastoral planning. The author stresses that participation is more valuable than producing a plan.

KNUDSEN, Raymond B. *New Models for Church Administration: The Practical Application of Business Principles.* Chicago: Association Press, 1979. 165pp.

This is the third in a series of new models books which the author applies to the administration of the local church. After introducing the book with a chapter comparing the common elements of business and religion, he treats long-range planning, funding, budgeting, stewardship, staffing and leadership.

MAVIS, W. Curry. *Advancing . . . the Smaller Church.* Grand Rapids: Baker Book House, 1968. 180pp.

The author writes about the urban and rural church with fewer than 150 members. He discusses principles which underlie effective work in these churches. He treats such topics as planning, organizing, budgeting, public relations, worship and education.

McCONKEY, Dale D. *Goal Setting: A Guide to Achieving the Church's Mission.* Minneapolis: Augsburg, 1978. 32pp.

This modest work deals with goal setting in a practical way. It defines, describes and illustrates the meaning of goals and the process of establishing them.

ODOM, Randall Young. *A Study of Environment, Strategy and Planning Processes in Churches.* Unpublished Ph.D. dissertation: University of Mississippi, 1984.

This is the author's dissertation for the Ph.D. in Business Administration. "The purpose of the study was to determine if churches pursue strategies and to investigate the relationship between strategies, organizational environments, and the extent of planning completeness and sophistication within church organizations" (p 21). The author surveyed literature on planning and strategy models. He surveyed churches in the Arkansas Baptist State Convention.

PAGE, Harry Robert. *Church Budget Development.* Englewood Cliffs, NJ: Prentice-Hall, 1964. 192pp.

This book aims at increasing effectiveness in planning and controlling the financial resources of the individual church. Budget development and use are treated as an administrative process common to churches of all denominations and sizes. This volume describes the underlying purposes of budgeting, its advantages and limitations, and its relationship to programs and future plans of the church. The entire budgeting process is explained and various techniques are explored. (Author's preface).

POPE, George M. and Bernard Quinn. *Planning for Planning.* Washington, D.C: Center for Applied Research in the Apostolate, 1972. 58pp.

This is a collection of papers presented at a conference of Catholic diocesan researchers and planners in 1972. There are three papers describing the activities of researching and planning in an individual diocese. The other papers address the themes of theology, implementation, methodology and relationships with other diocesan agencies.

RUSBULDT, Richard E. *Basic Leader Skills: Handbook for Church Leaders.* Valley Forge: Judson Press, 1981. 63pp.

The handbook for lay leadership is divided into five chapters: who is a leader, styles of leadership, functions of a leader, effective church planning and managing conflict. Each chapter explains the theory and gives exercises for the group to do. The last ten pages are a guide for those who would be leading the training sessions.

RUSBULDT, Richard E., Richard K. Gladden and Norman M. Green. *Key Steps in Local Church Planning.* Valley Forge, Pa: Judson Press, 1980. 106pp.

This volume is a digest of the key parts of the authors' 248-page LOCAL CHURCH PLANNING MANUAL. (1977). It is meant to be used independently or with the larger book.

RUSBULDT, Richard E., Richard K. Gladden and Norman M. Green, Jr. *Local Church Planning Manual.* Valley Forge, PA: Judson, 1977. 248pp.

This manual is designed to assist a congregation in its planning. It is written as a practical tool. With definitions, illustrations and steps, it will lead a planning group from writing the purpose statement to goal setting, mission design, mission management and finally, evaluation. The authors have included also 150 pages of appendixes.

RUSH, Myron D. *Management: A Biblical Approach.* Wheaton, IL: Victor, 1983. 236pp.

This book is designed to provide the principles of management outlined in the bible. It also supplies the leadership and management tools needed to apply these biblical principles of management successfully. The author is the owner of a manufacturing firm and a consultant for business firms and christian organizations. He attemps to write for the christian businessman as well as the church leader. There is a chapter on team spirit, planning, decision-making, communication skills, delegation, time management, conflict, and the christian manager's role in society.

SCHALLER, Lyle E. and Charles A. Tidwell. *Creative Church Administration.* Nashville: Abingdon, 1975. 208pp.

This book attempts to address the issue of church management from the point of view of creativity. The first chapter discusses the values which influence the creativity of the leader. This initial chapter is devoted to suggesting how the organizational structure can be altered to increase participation, enthusiasm, creativity, and openness to innovation. The second chapter presents different planning models. The remaining chapters are on motivation, volunteers, listening, recruitment, salaries, and evaluation.

SCHALLER, Lyle E. *Effective Church Planning.* Nashville: Abingdon, 1979. 176pp.

This book is intended to assist the pastor in problem-solving. The basic assumption in these pages is that people can resolve problems well if they have an accurate diagnosis of the nature of the situation. The author teaches how to identify and deal with the underlying factors which have low visibility but high impact on the dynamics of parish life. From this perspective the book deals with worship space, budgeting, evangelism, tenure and fellowship.

SCHALLER, Lyle E. *Looking in the Mirror: Self-Appraisal in the Local Church.* Nashville: Abingdon, 1984. 206pp.

The central goal of this book is to help congregational leaders expand their conceptual framework and ask new questions in self-appraisal efforts. The first four chapters raise broad general questions about the distinctive nature of the worshiping congregations. The next seven chapters focus on various aspects of congregational life ranging from the turning points of the past to the characteristics of today's members to the conceptual framework for program planning. The last three chapters raise questions that frequently are overlooked about youth ministries, nursery schools and the building planning committee.

SCHALLER, Lyle E. *Parish Planning.* Nashville: Abingdon, 1971. 239pp.

The author believes that a local church behaves like an institution. Therefore the church planning process would be assisted by the wisdom and experiences of organizational planners. This book suggests some approaches to parish planning from an institutional perspective. The topics treated are the budget, institutional blight, self-evaluation and accountability.

SCHALLER, Lyle E. *Planning for Protestantism in Urban America.* Nashville: Abingdon, 1965. 217pp.

This book is written from the perspective that planning is a process in which everyone who has a voice as a decision maker participates. The author begins with a case study. He then treats external assumptions, the theology of planning, planning interdenominationally, inner city planning and urban planning for churches.

SMITH, H. Paul and Ezra Earl Jones. *The Church Building Process.* Cincinnati: United Methodist Development Fund, 1975. 39pp.

The purpose of this booklet is to provide an overview of steps to be followed in building a church. Detailed information is not provided. There is information on preliminary planning, site selection, choosing an architect, construction and financing. The authors are experienced pastoral administrators.

STILES, Joseph. *Acquiring and Developing Church Real Estate.* Englewood Cliffs: Prentice-Hall, 1965. 189pp.

This book treats the topic of purchasing and developing property for the use of a local congregation. It explains the necessary steps of appointing a building commitee, studying and planning, working with an architect, fund-raising and other topics. The author, a businessman and university professor, was director of the Center for Church Business Management.

TAYLOR, Robert C. *How To Maintain Your Church Buildings and Grounds.* Westwood, NJ: Fleming H. Revell Co, 1962. 63pp.

A past officer of the American Society for Church Architecture, the author has served as designer and consultant for a number of new and renovated churches. He writes from his experience about how to set up a program of maintenance for churches. He treats the topics of record keeping, inventory and inspection, financial planning, project timing and delegation.

Theology, News and Notes-Alumni Newsletter. Pasadena, CA: Fuller Theological Seminary, 1973. 23pp.

This little booklet reprints seven articles on the topic of management in the church which appeared in earlier newsletters. The authors are experienced and recognized experts. They explain their ideas in goal setting, priorities, planning and motivation.

TIDWELL, Charles A. *Working Together through the Church Council.* Nashville: Convention Press, 1968. 114pp.

The church council of the Southern Baptist Convention is an advisory body which is involved in planning, coordinating and evaluating church programs and services. The author, an associate professor of church administration, explains every aspect of this council: how to form one, how to conduct a council meeting, how the council plans, coordinates and evaluates church programs. This book is written for use in a study group.

TUCKER, Grayson L., Jr. *A Church Planning Questionnaire.* c. 1982. 145pp.

This volume addresses the question: should I construct a questionnaire for my church. The author has not only done so successfully, but he has analyzed the outcomes. All the details about samples, tabulating and mailing are found here. The questionnaire is a tool for church planning.

WAGNER, C. Peter. *Leading Your Church Growth.* Ventura, CA: Regal Books, 1984. 224pp.

This is a book about leadership for church membership growth. The author explores the question: Why does a strong leadership influence positive growth? He addresses the leader as enabler, the art of followership, calling the right pastor and planning effective outreach.

WALRATH, Douglas A. *Planning for Your Church*. Philadelphia: Westminster Press, 1984. 112pp.

This work describes ways and means of effective long-range planning within a congregation. The author uses a team approach and emphasizes basic planning which sets overall goals and fashions programs to accomplish the goals. After focusing on the minister's own style of leadership and the choice of the planning committee, he looks at the process of community analysis. He then shows how to establish priorities and achieve consensus for a plan of action. The author is professor of Pastoral Studies at Bangor Theological Seminary.

WHEELEY, B. Otto and T. Cable. *Church Planning and Management*. Philadelphia: Dorrance and Co, 1975. 218pp.

The authors, industrial executives and members of Baptist congregations, write about the basic principles of management applied to all protestant churches. The volume is a handbook for local congregations. The chapters on planning, organization, constitutions, finances, education, recreation, worship and promotional methods are general, practical and accompanied by charts.

WHITE, Ray L. *How To Get Things Done*. Salt Lake City: Bookcraft, 1968. 164pp.

The author, a leader in the Church of Jesus Christ of Latter-day Saints, writes about the theory and practice of leadership for the believer. He covers planning, decision-making, and delegation. He gives practical hints on how to run a meeting and how to involve more people in the life of the church. It is aimed at the church membership who are all leaders.

WHITE. Robert N., ed. *Managing Today's* Church. Valley Forge: Judson, 1981. 192pp.

This book comes out of five years of church management seminars held at the Babcock Graduate School of Management of Wake Forest University. The authors are sem nar faculty members. They write about the fundamentals of management in a church environment. There is a chapter on the role and duties of the pastor. Planning is treated in three chapters (strategic, short-term and annual financial planning). After the chapter on marketing, three chapters follow on human resource management. The final chapter is on time management.

WIEST, Elam G. *How to Organize Your Church Staff.* Westwood, N.J.: Fleming H. Revell Co, 1962. 63pp.

This book aims at helping the pastor become a more effective administrator of church staff. Consideration is given to both professional as well as volunteer staff. The author treats such topics as the purpose of church organization, planning, problem-solving, titles, job descriptions and evaluations.

WILLIAMS, George M. *Improving Parish Management.* Mystic, CN: Twenty-Third Publications, 1983. 98pp.

The author, a retired businessman, writes about the fundamentals of managing a parish from the Catholic experience. He treats such topics as planning, organizing, training, delegating, managing volunteers, scheduling and running effective meetings.

WILSON, Charles R. *The Planning/Organization Workbook.* Arvada, CO: Jethro Publications, 1971.

The workbook (3-ring binder) is a system of strategic planning and management for non-profit organizations, especially churches. It contains seven sections covering the main topics of organizational management (e.g. mission, environment, goals, programs, etc.). The workbook instructs the user to collect information under the appropriate heading in order to make good planning decisions and decisions for action.

CHAPTER EIGHT

Staff Management

ADAMS, Arthur Merrihew. *Effective Leadership for Today's Church.* Philadelphia: Westminster Press, 1978. 190pp.

The author is an experienced Presbyterian pastor and professor at Princeton Theological Seminary. He intends this book for pastors and church officers. After two chapters on the spiritual role of the pastors, the following chapters treat the topics of authority, leadership styles, organizations, communications, planning and staff relationships.

BEHRING, Mark C. *A Strategy for Growth at Zion Lutheran Church Through Pastoral Leadership and Leadership Development.* Unpublished D.Min. Dissertation: Fuller Theological Seminary, 1985. 196+pp.

This is a study of pastoral leadership and its application to Zion Lutheran, whose pastor is the author. After a theological treatise on ministry, leadership and growth, this Doctor of Ministry dissertation treats pastoral leadership from the point of view of the pastor, the staff and lay leadership. The annual leadership retreat and a working plan for intentional leadership concludes the work.

BERGER, Hilbert J. *Time to Negotiate: Guidelines for Pastors to Follow When Salary Support is Considered.* New York: Friendship Press, 1973. 56pp.

This book was written for pastors who must negotiate their salaries with lay boards. The author, an experienced pastor, lays down the principles of such negotiation and outlines a method. While aimed as a tool for pastors, it also serves as a guide for lay committees.

ENGSTROM, Ted W. and Edward R. Dayton. *The Art of Management for Christian Leaders.* Waco, TX: Word Books, 1976. 285+pp.

This book contains both theory and practice. It treats the question of the nature of christian leadership and how it differs from secular organizations. The authors, well known for their publications, write about planning, leadership skills, hiring staff and managing time, meetings and interruptions.

GRAVES, Allen W. *Using and Maintaining Church Property.*
Englewood Cliffs, NJ: Prentice-Hall, 1965. 255pp.

"The book provides to church maintenance personnel.... an
understanding of many different facets of their work in readily
available form. This volume can guide church officials in
establishing proper administrative policies and in providing
needed supervision to secure quality performance."
"Maintenance" is used to include the operation of the building as
well as its protection. (From the author's preface).

GRAY, Gary M. *The Church Management Profession: A Descriptive
Analysis.* Minneapolis: National Association of Church Business
Administrators, 1970. 116pp.

This doctoral dissertation studies the profession of church
management. The following questions were researched and
analyzed in this study: Who is serving in this role of managers?
What churches employ these people? Where are they? How do
members of the National Association of Church Business
Administrators compare to church managers who are not
members?.

GRAY, Rhea, et al. *Experiences in Activating Congregations: A Cross
Denominational Study.* Chicago: Institute for Ministry
Development, 1978. 114pp.

This is a report of an action-research project to study theory and
practice for revitalizing churches. It is intended to be helpful to
church leaders, judicatory officials, national program agency staff
and consultants. This study brought together a psychological
tradition which emphasized voluntary behavioral change and
achievement motivation and a wholistic organizational approach
to congregations which emphasized the contributions of classical
organizational theory as well as more contemporary theories and
methods (including Etzioni's theory of activation). The church
communities studied were Roman Catholic, Lutheran and
Presbyterian. (from the Preface.).

HOLCK, Manfred, Jr. *Clergy Desk Book.* Nashville: Abingdon, 1985. 288pp.

This is a book for parish pastors. It treats the major topics of church administration: ministers as managers and leaders, organizing the church, staff, volunteers, programming, property and plant, communications, salary, bookkeeping, fund-raising, computers, membership recruitment and taxes. It is meant to be a practical help so sample forms and charts are included. It has a small bibliography and helpful index.

HOWSE, W. L. *The Church Staff and Its Work.* Nashville: Broadman, 1959. 174pp.

The author, a member of the Southern Baptist Church, explains the role of each key staff person in a church. His focus is the educational ministry. He addresses the leadership qualifications of staff members and methods of developing leadership.

JUDY, Marvin T. *The Multiple Staff Ministry.* Nashville: Abingdon, 1969. 287pp.

This book is the result of extensive research and accumulation of data from 1400 churches representing 22 denominations. This work contains theoretical material (theology, sociology, etc.), analytical material (statistics) and practical material (administrative procedures). After introductory chapters on leadership, personnel management and group dynamics, the author treats each position found in churches with multiple staffs.

NEWSOME, Robert R. *The Ministering Parish: Methods and Procedures for the Pastoral Organization.* New York: Paulist Press, 1982. 101pp.

This book is the result of grass-roots work done by the Parish Corporate Renewal Network in Chicago and the Pastoral Alliance for Corporate Renewal in Toledo. The four facets of parish renewal which are treated in this volume are: vision, staff development, structures and ministry. The intent of this work is not simply to educate the laity but to establish a mutual grouping in a deep sense of communion out of which life and service together flow. The author is a clinical psychologist specializing in organizational development and human resources training.

OLSEN, Frank H. *Church Staff Support: Cultivating and Maintaining Staff Relationships.* Minneapolis: Augsburg, 1982. 39pp.

Pastors and lay professionals need support. They need someone to lean on and share their concerns with. This book describes the need for this support and offers a model for establishing a staff support group. It outlines the purposes and objectives of such a group and lists the benefits which will be derived.

SCHALLER, Lyle E. *The Multiple Staff and the Larger Church.* Nashville: Abingdon, 1980. 142pp.

While the number of large (800-1,000 members) churches is relatively small (5-7% of each denomination) they are different from the smaller congregations. This book addresses those differences. There are chapters on the staffing question, the senior minister and the associate minister.

SWEET, Herman J. *The Multiple Staff in the Local Church.* Philadelphia: Westminster Press, 1963. 122pp.

The author has served in several United Presbyterian churches which had multiple staffs. His experience is the subject matter of this book. He treats the issue of recruiting, maintaining and evaluating staff members. He discusses the difference between a well organized and a more charismatic church.

WEDEL, Leonard E. *Building and Maintaining a Church Staff.* Nashville: Broadman, 1966. 158pp.

This is a practical book about managing church staff. The author writes about advertising for a job, interviewing, helping a new employee get a good start, organizing the jobs, just wages, supervising and the role of the personnel committee. The book is written from the experience of the author and he does not use any references.

WEDEL, Leonard E. *Church Staff Administration.* Nashville: Broadmann, 1978. 193pp.

This volume is a revision of the author's earlier work: Building and Maintaining a Church Staff. It treats the issue of personnel in a local church from a practical viewpoint. The author, an experienced pastor, writes about selecting, training and organizing church employees. He proposes a formal salary plan, gives the elements of job descriptions and discusses supervisory skills. The last chapters treat how to conduct staff meetings and the role of the church personnel committee.

WESTING, Harold J. *Multiple Church Staff Handbook*. Grand Rapids: Kregel Publications, 1985. 208pp.

The larger churches have several staff members. The book describes the work done by a multiple staff and gives practical advice for improving staff effectiveness. The author, associate professor of Christian Education at Conservative Baptist Seminary in Denver, begins by describing the goal of the staff as a team. He then treats the various ways the team functions. Finally he talks about the means used to maintain a successful team.

WIEST, Elam G. *How to Organize Your Church Staff*. Westwood, N.J.: Fleming H. Revell Co, 1962. 63pp.

This book aims at helping the pastor become a more effective administrator of church staff. Consideration is given to both professional as well as volunteer staff. The author treats such topics as the purpose of church organization, planning, problem-solving, titles, job descriptions and evaluations.

WILLIAMS, Denny. *Leadership Life-Style*. Kansas City, MO: Beacon Hill Press, 1983. 120pp.

The author, an ordained minister and a doctor of business administration, explains the basic principles of staff management. He directs his writing to the pastor and others who have positions of leadership in the local church. This volume is divided into six main headings. Each heading contains many topics which cover, on average, two pages. Every aspect of parish administration, organization, personnel service, advertising and office management is treated in practical fashion.

CHAPTER NINE

Studies of Specific Churches

ALLRED, Thurman W. *Basic Small Church Administration.* Nashville: Convention Press, 1981. 64pp.

This is a practical "how-to" book aimed at pastors of small, rural churches having Southern Baptist affiliation. The authors are mostly experienced pastors who discuss skills such as administration, programming, decision-making, planning and budgeting.

ANDERSON, James D. *To Come Alive!* San Francisco: Harper & Row, 1973. 141pp.

The author, a church planner, shares what he has learned about member motivation, sources of power, utilization of conflict, leadership and management of change. A blend of theology and behavioral science theory, this book is filled with examples and case studies. It offers practical suggestions to reorganize congregational structures.

ASHEIM, Ivar and Victor R. Gold, eds. *Episcopacy in the Lutheran Church: Studies in the Development and Definition of the Office of Church Leadership.* Philadelphia: Fortress Press, 1970. 261pp.

This is a historical and theological study of the development and meaning of the office of leader in the Lutheran Church. By tracing historical lines and transitions over time and cultures, it attempts to give the younger churches of Asia and Africa some assistance in answering the questions about what must be held constant and what can be adapted to local conditions.

BAXTER, Nathan Dwight. *Four Cases and Teaching Resources to Enable Religious Leaders to be More Subjectively and Theoretically Aware in Parish Conflict Situations.* Unpublished D.Min. Dissertation: Lancaster Theological Seminary, 1985. 183pp.

This Doctor of Ministry dissertation contains four case studies in the subject of conflict in the parish. The areas of conflict are: negotiating for self-interest; parish community relations; organizational subsystems; pastoral care. After each case there is a section on teaching the case and a section on goals and resources.

BEHRING, Mark C. *A Strategy for Growth at Zion Lutheran Church Through Pastoral Leadership and Leadership Development.* Unpublished D.Min. Dissertation: Fuller Theological Seminary, 1985. 196+pp.

This is a study of pastoral leadership and its application to Zion Lutheran, whose pastor is the author. After a theological treatise on ministry, leadership and growth, this Doctor of Ministry dissertation treats pastoral leadership from the point of view of the pastor, the staff and lay leadership. The annual leadership retreat and a working plan for intentional leadership concludes the work.

BEVERIDGE, Wilbert E. *Managing the Church.* Naperville, IL: SCM Book Club, 1971. 124pp.

The author, a member of the department of Management Studies at Middlesex Polytechnic, writes from his British experience and point of view. He discusses the nature and structure of groups and various organizations using the findings of behavioral science. He applies this knowledge to the church. He concentrates on how "management by objectives" can be used effectively in parishes and specialized ministries (e.g. industrial chaplaincies).

BREKKE, Milo, Merton Strommen and Dorothy Williams. *Ten Faces of Ministry.* Minneapolis: Augsburg, 1979. 256pp.

This book reports the findings of a comprehensive study of the Lutheran church. 5000 Lutherans were surveyed on the topic of ministry. This book, then, contains the results of this questionnaire. The first five chapters treat five different areas of ministerial perspective. The next five chapters treat areas of skill and performance.

CARROLL, Jackson W., ed. *Small Churches Are Beautiful.* New York: Harper & Row, 1977. 174pp.

In the world of "bigger is better" is there a place for a small church? This collection of essays not only answers positively but gives expert advice on how to organize, plan, develop, and allocate resources in a small church. The context for these reflections is a Protestant denomination of under 200 members.

DIETTERICH, Paul M., ed. *Clergy Growth and Church Vitalization.* Naperville: Center for Parish Development, 1977. 184pp.

This is the fifth report in Experiment in District Revitalization of the United Methodist Church. The purpose of this report is to explore the role of the pastor as the person in the local church who is in the best position to enable the vitalization of the church. This report explores the nature of the effective practice of ministry and how to equip persons for that ministry.

DOOHAN, Helen. *Leadership in Paul.* Wilmington, DE: Michael Glazier, 1984. 208pp.

Starting with the premise that understanding the scriptures is necessary for understanding christian leadership, this study of Pauline writing examines leadership in the early church. The author, assistant professor of Religious Studies at Gonzaga University, presents the social and religious environment of each Pauline letter and shows the style of leadership used to solve conflicts and direct the development of the christian communities.

DUDLEY, Carl S. ed. *Building Effective Ministry: Theory and Practice in the Local Church.* San Francisco: Harper & Row, 1983. 267pp.

The purpose of this collection of essays is to provide new avenues into the social and spiritual dynamics of a local church. The book is a series of reflections on a "case". The first set of reflections are written from the vantage point of academic disciplines. The next set, from the point of view of church consultants. The final set of reflections attempts to integrate the various approaches.

DUDLEY, Carl S. *Making the Small Church Effective.* Nashville: Abingdon, 1978. 192pp.

This book tells the story of the small and effective congregation. From years of study and giving workshops the author analyzes the strengths of the small church and explains the dynamics that have been proven successful. He offers helpful resources, practical exercises and tested tools to those charged with the leadership of these congregations.

GOODMAN, Grace A. *Rocking the Ark.* New York: United
Presbyterian Church, 1968. 214pp.

These nine case studies demonstrate how some churches have
renewed themselves. These cases were first used during a series
of consultations conducted by the Division of Evangelism of the
Presbyterian Church. Each case studies a church of different size
and different environment. The author concludes the book with
questions and her observations.

GORMAN, James C. *Explorations into the Work of the Roman Catholic
Parish Priest: A Managerial and Administrative Focus.* Unpublished
Ph.D. dissertation: Brandeis University, 1978. 468 [leaves].

This is a study of the work of Catholic diocesan parish priests. The
study focuses on the needs and concerns of church administrators
and managers, namely the concerns of job design and redesign,
education and training, personal selection, supervision and
evaluation. This doctoral dissertation measured the activities of
priests and their impact on the priests' work behavior.

GRAY, Gary M. *The Church Management Profession: A Descriptive
Analysis.* Minneapolis: National Association of Church Business
Administrators, 1970. 116pp.

This doctoral dissertation studies the profession of church
management. The following questions were researched and
analyzed in this study: Who is serving in this role of managers?
What churches employ these people? Where are they? How do
members of the National Association of Church Business
Administrators compare to church managers who are not
members?

GREENLEAF, Robert K. *The Servant as Religious Leader.* Peterborough,
NH: Center for Applied Studies, 1982. 56pp.

This monograph is the latest in a series written by this author. The
purpose of this work is to increase the number of capable and
motivated religious leaders. The first sections are dedicated to
describing the leader and examining some examples. There is a
section on teaching leadership in seminaries. The last sections deal
with pitfalls and new frontiers.

HALL, Douglas T. and Benjamin Schneider. *Organizational Climates and Careers: The Work Lives of Priests*. New York: Seminar Press, 1973. 291pp.

This is the report on the behavioral science diagnosis of the Catholic Archdiocese of Hartford. There were three major purposes of the study: to present a theory of career development in organizations which draw on a number of social and behavioral science disciplines and which work under clearly and uniquely defined organizational conditions: Catholic diocesan priests; and to study intensively the careers of priests as a distinctive group of working men. The study indirectly addresses some issues about leadership experiences and skills.

HEAD, Robert F. *Essentials of Church Administration*. Poplar Bluff, MO: General Baptist Press, 1966. 137pp.

This work on Baptist Church administration contains chapters on organization and officials, cooperative responsibilities (e.g., relationship between the local church and national associations), ministry, auxiliaries and their functions, coordination of the total church program, the pastor as administrator, and church growth.

HOWSE, W. L. and W. O. Thomason. *A Church Organized and Functioning*. Nashville: Convention Press, 1963. 148pp.

This work is the result of information gathered from twenty-one Baptist churches regarding their function. The book is organized as a text for classroom use. It is intended for those who wish more knowledge about the organization of the church and its leadership roles.

JOHNSON, Luke T. *Decision Making in the Church: A Biblical Model*. Philadelphia: Fortress Press, 1983. 109pp.

There should be a close connection between what a group claims to be and the way it does things. This is the basic premise of the author, associate professor of religious studies at Indiana University. He examines the nature of decision making and the many New Testament texts which treat decisions. He leads the reader to the understanding that a community of faith needs to make decisions in correspondence with the theology it believes in. Finally, he suggests a model for a truly pastoral and theological way of making decisions true to scripture, tradition and experience.

LEAS, Speed B. *Time Management.* Nashville: Abingdon, 1978. 123pp.

This volume explains how church leaders must take the initiative if they are to be good stewards of the hours given by God to them. A good leader cannot passively accept the demands placed by others. The leader must set priorities and allocate time. The author does not simply list "oughts" but the "laws" to use time creatively and effectively. The compulsive worker and the procrastinator are described and used as case studies.

LEHMAN, Edward. *Breaking Through the Gender Barriers.* New Brunswick: Transition Books, 1985. 307pp.

This book presents the results of a series of research projects which the author conducted in conjuction with the United Presbyterian Church. One survey measured receptivity to women as clergy. Another evaluated the performance of clergywomen. The third study collected data from the clergywomen themselves. The author has written for those who have no social science background. (From a review by Helen Ebaugh.).

LEIFFER, Murray H. *What District Superintendents Say or The District Superintendent in the Methodist Church.* Evanston, Il: Bureau of Social and Religious Research, 1971. 194pp.

This is a study of the job of the District Superintendents of the United Methodist Church. 478 superintendents were the subjects of the study. The book contains text of interpretation and implication. It also has the charts of results from the questionnaire. Many items are applicable to similar positions in other churches.

LEWIS, Larry L. *Organize to Evangelize: A Manual for Church Growth.* Wheaton, IL: Victor Books, 1980. 132pp.

This book examines and explains the various steps in the time-honored Flake Formula for church growth, named after Arthur Flake. The author demonstrates its effectiveness by showing how well it worked in three distinct settings, the last being Tower Grove Baptist Church in St Louis where he was pastor.

MASSEY, Floyd, Jr. and Samuel Berry McKinney. *Church Administration in the Black Perspective.* Valley Forge, PA: Judson Press, 1976. 172pp.

This book speaks to the administration of black Baptist Churches. The black church constituency is composed of the organized poor, who lack financial resources and the power to change their condition. The authors have set forth guidelines for developing effective organization of the church, boards, and committees. They show how the African heritage and the slave experience have molded traditions which are significant in black church life today.

MICKEY, Paul A. and Robert L. Wilson. *Conflict and Resolution.* Nashville: Abingdon, 1973. 160pp.

This book uses case studies to examine the issues of conflict between individuals and groups in the church. After a chapter on the theological and psychological principles of conflict, there is a series of short case studies with discussion questions designed to highlight the basic issues involved. No decisions or solutions are offered.

O'BRIEN, Gary Donald. *Developing a Collegial Style of Leadership: Sharing Responsibility in the Local Religious Community.* Unpublished D.Min. dissertation: The Catholic University of America, 1984. 203pp.

In this Catholic University Doctor of Ministry dissertation, the author studies the principles and dynamics of a collegial style of leadership. Using the research of Rensis Likert, the author actually conducted a project of developing and implementing a collegial model of leadership in a religious community retreat house. The heart of the project was a three-day workshop on this style of leadership. This dissertation reports on the method and results of the project.

PHILLIPS, Harold R. and Robert E. Firth. *Cases in Denominational Administration: A Management Casebook for Decision-making.* Berrier Springs, MI: Andrews University Press, 1978. 314pp.

As the title indicates, this book is a collection of cases chosen to show the kinds of problems with which church administrators must grapple. The cases are grouped in the following sections: church institutions, church operated commercial enterprises, conference organizations, local churches and pastoral problems and personal and personnel problems. The last two sections will appeal to seminars, study groups and classes. The first section focuses more on decisions to be made in business related situations. The book begins with two chapters explaining how to analyze a case.

RUDGE, Peter F. *Ministry and Management.* London: Travistock Publications, 1968. 191pp.

This book reflects the author's experience as a minister in the Church of England and his management studies. The first section describes five theories of administration and examines their theological implications. The next section investigates these same theories as they are practiced in ecclesiastical administration.

SAFRANSKI, Scott R. *Managing God's Organization: The Catholic Church in Society.* Ann Arbor, MI: UMI Research Press, 1985. 199pp.

This volume is the revision of the author's doctoral dissertation. It studies the Catholic Church from an organizational, not theological perspective. The focus is the interaction of units, at various levels of the church's hierarchy, with groups outside the church. Church organization and management processes are then studied in terms of adaptations made in an effort to assume cooperation and stable relationships with important internal and external interest groups and resource suppliers. The work contains the results of an empirical case study in which the resource dependence model was applied to one archdiocese.

SHAWCHUCK, Norman. *What It Means To Be a Church Leader.* Indianapolis: Spiritual Growth Resources, 1984. 71pp.

The author studies three topics from a biblical and theological perspective: appropriate ministry styles, the "seasons" which come to a congregation and the necessity of adapting one's ministry style according to the "seasons." The three topics of ministry found in the bible are priest, prophet and king. The author believes that each congregation today needs the same three ministry styles: priest, prophet and organizational leader.

SMITH, Rockwell, ed. *Sociological Studies of an Occupation: The Ministry.* Roswell, NM: Hall-Poorbaugh Press, 1979. 68pp.

Four areas of ministry practices researched by extensive use of questionnaires. The areas are: the ministry of the laity, women in ministry, conflicting perspectives on the minister's role and supervision of the minister. The study was conducted by the Leiffer Bureau of Social Religious Research on the Illinois United Methodist Church.

STATON, Knofel. *God's Plan for Church Leadership.* Cincinnati: Standard Publishing, 1982. 155pp.

The author studies the biblical principles and corresponding practices that he judges are essential for effective christian leadership. The leadership of Jesus is explained. There are chapters on Paul, Barnabas, the apostles, the pastors, and the elders. The final chapters analyze the biblical findings.

STONE, Sam E. *The Christian Minister.* Cincinnati: Standard Publishing, 1980. 252pp.

The author examines the role of the minister in the bible and in the present church. He studies the minister's personal life, his relationships and his job. In the last section, the topics include preaching, counseling, administration and conducting services. Each chapter contains questions to think about, a list of additional resources, and project ideas.

SWEETSER, Thomas P. *The Catholic Parish.* Chicago: Center for the Scientific Study of Religion, 1974. 134pp.

This book deals with shifting membership patterns in the American Catholic parish since Vatican II. The purpose of this volume is to provide information based on a group of Catholic parishes which can be used as a comparison for other parish situations. Eight suburban communities with ten parishes were studied. There is a chapter on each of the following topics: the response of the clergy, the reaction of the laity, the function and role of a Catholic parish and finally, the reasons for changing membership.

WALKER, Joe W. *Money in the Church.* Nashville: Abingdon, 1982. 125pp.

"I believe talking about money in the church is holy talk, deeply theological, and as sacred as prayer." So says the author of this volume which examines the part money plays in the United Methodist Church. He reports on the past and present patterns of giving. He studies the motivation used in collecting money and the motives which move Methodists to give. The book concludes with a discussion of the financial pressures facing the denomination and offers some methods to meet these challenges.

WALRATH, Douglas A. *Leading Churches Through Change.* Nashville: Abingdon, 1979. 124pp.

This is a collection of six case studies of churches and change. In each case the author explains the problem, the solution and applications to other situations. The author is a church development consultant who formerly served as an executive with the Reformed Church in America.

WALRATH, Douglas A. *Planning for Your Church.* Philadelphia: Westminster Press, 1984. 112pp.

This work describes ways and means of effective long-range planning within a congregation. The author uses a team approach and emphasizes basic planning which sets overall goals and fashions programs to accomplish the goals. After focusing on the minister's own style of leadership and the choice of the planning committee, he looks at the process of community analysis. He then shows how to establish priorities and achieve consensus for a plan of action. The author is professor of Pastoral Studies at Bangor Theological Seminary.

CHAPTER TEN

Theological and Biblical Perspectives

ADAMS, Arthur Merrihew. *Effective Leadership for Today's Church.* Philadelphia: Westminster Press, 1978. 190pp.

The author is an experienced Presbyterian pastor and professor at Princeton Theological Seminary. He intends this book for pastors and church officers. After two chapters on the spiritual role of the pastors, the following chapters treat the topics of authority, leadership styles, organizations, communications, planning and staff relationships.

ANDERSON, Ray S. *Minding God's Business.* Grand Rapids: Wm. Eerdmans Publishing Co, 1986. 156pp.

The author is professor of theology and ministry at Fuller Theological Seminary and a lecturer in the Institute for Christian Organizational Development there. He presents a biblical and theological basis for understanding the unique characteristics of christian organizations and what it means to manage them in a christian way. He discusses the role of leadership in managing christian organizations and addresses such issues as strategic planning, mission statements and ethical questions facing the leader.

ASHEIM, Ivar and Victor R. Gold, eds. *Episcopacy in the Lutheran Church: Studies in the Development and Definition of the Office of Church Leadership.* Philadelphia: Fortress Press, 1970. 261pp.

This is a historical and theological study of the development and meaning of the office of leader in the Lutheran Church. By tracing historical lines and transitions over time and cultures, it attempts to give the younger churches of Asia and Africa some assistance in answering the questions about what must be held constant and what can be adapted to local conditions.

BARRS, Jerram. *Shepherds and Sheep: A Biblical View of Leading and Following.* Downers Grove, IL: InterVarsity Press, 1983. 98pp.

This is a biblical critique of common leadership patterns which the author has identified in various church groups. By recalling the New Testament doctrine of the priesthood of believers, Christians will avoid current abuses of shepherding and eldership, especially the trend toward leadership to assume more authority than God intends.

BAXTER, Nathan Dwight. *Four Cases and Teaching Resources to Enable Religious Leaders to be More Subjectively and Theoretically Aware in Parish Conflict Situations.* Unpublished D.Min. Dissertation: Lancaster Theological Seminary, 1985. 183pp.

This Doctor of Ministry dissertation contains four case studies in the subject of conflict in the parish. The areas of conflict are: negotiating for self-interest; parish community relations; organizational subsystems; pastoral care. After each case there is a section on teaching the case and a section on goals and resources.

BEHRING, Mark C. *A Strategy for Growth at Zion Lutheran Church Through Pastoral Leadership and Leadership Development.* Unpublished D.Min. Dissertation: Fuller Theological Seminary, 1985. 196+pp.

This is a study of pastoral leadership and its application to Zion Lutheran, whose pastor is the author. After a theological treatise on ministry, leadership and growth, this Doctor of Ministry dissertation treats pastoral leadership from the point of view of the pastor, the staff and lay leadership. The annual leadership retreat and a working plan for intentional leadership concludes the work.

BELL, A. Donald. *How to Get Along with People in the Church.* Grand Rapids: Zondervan, 1960. 159pp.

The author believes that many church leaders are ineffective because they cannot get along with other people. He holds that there are three main sources of help for Christians with personality problems: the examples of Christ, the principles of applied psychology and the psychology of salesmanship. This book explains these sources and applies them to the church worker. Dr. Bell is professor of Psychology and Human Relations at Southwestern Baptist Theological Seminary. (From a review by A. Haze).

BOYAJIAN, Jane A., ed. *Ethical Issues in the Practice of Ministry.* Minneapolis: United Theological Seminary of the Twin Cities, 1984. 98pp.

This volume presents a rich ecumenical discussion of ethical issues in the work of ministry. Most of the authors first presented their ideas at the conference "Ethics and the Practice of Ministry" held in Minneapolis in 1981. After introductory chapters on philosophy and method, the book contains reflections on the ethics of preaching, social ministry, counselling and interim ministry.

BRATTGORD, Helge. *God's Stewards: A Theological Study of the Principles of Stewardship.* Trans. by Gene J. Lund. Minneapolis: Augsburg, 1963. 248pp.

The first half of this book examines the notion of stewardship in the scriptures. The second half analyzes the Lutheran confessions for a theology of stewardship. As a result of his study, the author, a Swedish theologian and minister, believes that stewardship is more than fund-raising. It is the care of all gifts given by God.

BREEN, David P. *Churches in Conflict: A Conflict Management Manual for Church Leaders.* Unpublished D.Min. dissertation: Western Theological Seminary, 1983. 134pp.

This four-unit manual is designed for church leaders as a guide to conflict management in the local congregation. It discusses a theory of organizational conflict and reports the results of a survey of church leaders in the Reformed Church of America on their responses to conflict. The manual explores the relationship between certain emotions and conflict and offers some scriptural and theological themes as resources.

BRIGGS, Edwin A., ed. *Theological Perspectives of Stewardship.* Evanston, Il: United Methodist Church, 1969. 165pp.

In the spring of 1967 a seminar on stewardship was held in Chicago. The Stewardship and Finance section of the United Methodist Church designed the seminar as a study to provide background for the formulation of a creed or foundation statement. The twelve lectures of the seminar form the chapters of this book.

BUTTON, Lewis I. *A Self-Description with Analysis of the Management Styles of Independent, Fundamental Pastors.* Eastern Baptist Theological Seminary: Unpublished D.Min. dissertation, 1983. 196pp.

As the title explains, this dissertation for the Doctor of Ministry at Eastern Baptist Theological Seminary reports the findings from a survey of pastors associated with the Independent Fundamental Churches of America. The leadership styles of these pastors are compared and contrasted with the study of leadership in the bible. There is also a short review of literature in church management.

CALIAN, Samuel Carnegie. *Today's Pastor in Tomorrow's World*. New York: Hawthorn, 1977. 153pp.

Building on the research of the Association of Theological Schools' Readiness for Ministry Project, the author identifies eight current models of ministry. After some evaluation of each, he proposes his model: the pastor as grass-roots theologian. He gives the scriptural and theological foundation for this model and applies it to several aspects of pastoral ministry.

CAMPBELL, Thomas C. and Gary B. Reierson. *The Gift of Administration*. Philadelphia: Westminster Press, 1981. 139pp.

Why do ministers have to be administrators? Because administration is a spiritual gift through which ministry happens. This is the thesis of this little book which started as a series of lectures by Campbell and was completed by Reierson. It is a scriptural and theological study of the administrative tasks of stewards, elders, bishops and deacons.

CORNWALL, Judson. *Profile of a Leader*. Plainfield, NJ: Logos International, 1980. 227pp.

Using the stories, parables and images of the bible, the author paints the picture of the minister as leader. These vignettes are grouped together to form four profiles: two are Old Testament similes; two are New Testament parables. Some of this material was previously published in three booklets.

CUNNINGHAM, Richard B. *Creative Stewardship*. Nashville: Abingdon, 1979. 128pp.

This little book contains guidelines for applying principles and patterns of christian stewardship. The author, associate professor of Christian Philosophy at Southern Baptist Theological Seminary, begins with the scriptural and theological meanings of stewardship. He then describes the process of good stewardship and ends with some thoughts on the corporate stewardship of the Church.

DALE, Robert D. *Ministers as Leaders.* Nashville: Broadman Press, 1984. 132pp.

This book explains leadership styles. It offers some theological reflections on various styles and gives examples on how to match leader and follower styles. The last section illustrates the interactive leadership style. The author is a professor of pastoral leadership and church ministries at Southeastern Baptist Seminary.

DALE, Robert D. *Pastoral Leadership.* Nashville: Abingdon Press, 1986. 240pp.

The author presents his ideas on the basis of pastoral leadership in a congregational setting. He describes pastoral leadership and gives some theological, biblical and philosophical bases for its understanding. He discusses leadership styles and the skills needed in a leader. The last chapters deal with personal issues facing a church leader.

DOBBINS, Gaines S. *A Ministering Church.* Nashville: Broadman Press, 1960. 231pp.

Beginning with an examination of the church's purpose, the author proceeds to demonstrate the need for multiple ministries working together to fulfil this purpose. The main theme is that a church pastor must be a leader and an administrator as well as a preacher and counselor. The author taught for three decades at the Southern Baptist Theological Seminary.

DOOHAN, Helen. *Leadership in Paul.* Wilmington, DE: Michael Glazier, 1984. 208pp.

Starting with the premise that understanding the scriptures is necessary for understanding christian leadership, this study of Pauline writing examines leadership in the early church. The author, assistant professor of Religious Studies at Gonzaga University, presents the social and religious environment of each Pauline letter and shows the style of leadership used to solve conflicts and direct the development of the christian communities.

EIMS, LeRoy. *Be the Leader You Were Meant To Be: What the Bible Says About Leadership.* Wheaton, IL: Victor Books, 1975. 132pp.

The author is director of evangelism for the Navigators. The book is an outgrowth of his personal study of the Scriptures and his work in training christian leaders. Each chapter presents a quality or characteristic of a christian leader as found in the bible, especially in the lives of biblical figures.

ENGSTROM, Ted W. *The Making of a Christian Leader.* Grand Rapids, MI: Zondervan, 1976.

This book was written according to the author "to help the christian leader get a clearer picture of what he wants to do and be in a church or organization." After three chapters exploring the scriptural teaching, the author explains the styles of leadership, the price of leadership and how to develop leadership skills. The final chapters treat motivation, planning and taking control.

FORD, George L. *Manual on Management for Christian Workers.* Grand Rapids: Zondervan, 1964. 152pp.

The author served sixteen years as a pastor and ten years as Executive Director of the National Association of Evangelicals. He writes from his experience and insight. This is a general treatment of the major themes of church management with strong influence from biblical literature. It is aimed at all christians who manage, but especially church administrators.

GANGEL, Kenneth O. *Competent to Lead.* Chicago: Moody Press, 1974. 144pp.

The purpose of this volume is to speak specifically to the issue of human relations in the church and its affiliate organizations. This is done by drawing principles from both similar research and biblical texts, in an effort to blend the two into a Christian philosophy of collective service and ministry. The audience is lay persons of the evangelical church who need to understand and practice professional administration.

GREELEY, Andrew et al. *Parish, Priest and People: New Leadership for the Local Church.* Chicago: Thomas More Press, 1981. 262pp.

This is an interdisciplinary study of pastoral leadership in the local church. This collaboration between social scientists and theologians reflects on various aspects of the local religious community (church). The second part examines the leadership of the local church, emphasizing the priestly function. The third section treats the issue of educating the religious leader especially in the skills of preaching.

GREENLEAF, Robert K. *The Servant as Religious Leader.* Peterborough, NH: Center for Applied Studies, 1982. 56pp.

This monograph is the latest in a series written by this author. The purpose of this work is to increase the number of capable and motivated religious leaders. The first sections are dedicated to describing the leader and examining some examples. There is a section on teaching leadership in seminaries. The last sections deal with pitfalls and new frontiers.

HALL, Douglas John. *The Steward: A Biblical Symbol Come of Age.* New York: Friendship Press for the Commission of Stewardship, NCC, 1982. 147pp.

This book provides the biblical background necessary to rethink, in the light of our contemporary situation, the origins of the idea of christian stewardship. This is done through reflection on the historical evolution of North American Church practice as it incorporated stewardship into its life and work. The author, a professor of Christian Theology at McGill University in Montreal, believes that we had lost the original meaning of stewardship. It is not a function of mission but mission is a function of stewardship! (From the bookjacket).

HARRELL, Costen J. *Stewardship and the Tithe.* New York: Abingdon, 1953. 61pp.

This book treats the christian doctrine of stewardship by addressing three issues: the biblical basis of stewardship, the theological teaching and the history and practice of tithing. The author indicated only a few of his sources.

HEYD, Thomas. *Planning for Stewardship*. Minneapolis: Augsburg, 1980. 40pp.

This is a practical book about developing a giving program for church congregations; after explaining the biblical meaning of stewardship, the author treats planning and organizing a stewardship program. There are five pages of exhibits.

HOLT, David R. *Handbook of Church Finance*. New York: Macmillan, 1960. 201pp.

Few areas of the church's life are more obscure than financial administration of the Lord's work. There has been interest in producing a body of sound stewardship literature based on a biblical understanding of divine ownership and the resultant cosmic relationship of God's people to God's property. The purpose of this study is to gather and report the results of a questionnaire on the need for a handbook in church finance and to write such a handbook. (From the Introduction).

HUDNUT, Robert K. *Arousing the Sleeping Giant: How to Organize Your Church For Action*. New York: Harper and Row, 1973. 186pp.

The author has applied the ideas and suggestions found in this book to St Luke Presbyterian Church in Minneapolis. He has written from the conviction that planning will make the church count for something. The book basically addresses the various aspects of planning for the local church. Several introductory chapters discuss the theological and biblical basis for planning.

JACKSON, B. F., Jr., ed. *Communication-Learning for Churchmen*. Nashville: Abingdon, 1968. 303pp.

This four part, four author book addresses the principles and practice of communications and learning. It describes the process from a theological perspective. It treats how to use print and audiovisual resources in the communication process.

JOHNSON, Luke T. *Decision Making in the Church: A Biblical Model.* Philadelphia: Fortress Press, 1983. 109pp.

There should be a close connection between what a group claims to be and the way it does things. This is the basic premise of the author, associate professor of religious studies at Indiana University. He examines the nature of decision making and the many New Testament texts which treat decisions. He leads the reader to the understanding that a community of faith needs to make decisions in correspondence with the theology it believes in. Finally, he suggests a model for a truly pastoral and theological way of making decisions true to scripture, tradition and experience.

JONES, Ezra Earl. *Strategies for New Churches.* New York: Harper and Row, 1976. 178pp.

"How do you go about organizing a new church in your community?" This book addresses the many facets of this question. The author first provides a historical, theological and sociological overview of the nature and function of the local church. He continues with the actual process of organizing new congregations. He analyzes the needs of various types of churches: suburban, special purpose, downtown and others. The author has been the associate director of research for the United Methodist Board of Global Ministries.

KUNTZ, Kenneth. *Wooden Chalices.* St. Louis: Bethany Press, 1963. 192pp.

This book on christian stewardship was written at the request of the stewardship committee of the Disciples of Christ Church. It is a collation of biblical passages, illustrations from literature and experience on the major experts of stewardship. It is intended as a resource for those who are required to give talks on this topic. The chapters of the book are written in the style of a meditation.

LINDGREN, Alvin J. *Foundations for Purposeful Church Administration.*
New York: Abingdon, 1965. 302pp.

"This is not a book about church administration but a guiding
statement for church administrations. The focus is upon preparing
the minister to be a church administrator by interpreting what
church administration is, the foundations on which it rests, and
the prerequisites for leadership in this field.... It will be strongly
emphasized throughout (the book) that at the basic foundation on
which all church administration rests is a clear understanding of
the christian faith and of the mission of the church." (From the
author's introduction) The author taught for many years at
Garrett Theological Seminary.

MacNAIN, Donald T. *The Growing Local Church.* Grand Rapids: Baker
Book House, 1975.

The author, a Presbyterian minister, has divided this work into
four parts. The first part is a biblical reflection on the church as an
organization. The second part deals with both the office and work
of the pastor-teacher. The third part treats the office and work of
various church officials. The final part discusses the decision
making and leadership role of the congregation.

McCARTT, Clara Anniss. *How to Organize Your Church Office.*
Westwood, NJ: Fleming H. Revell Co, 1962. 63pp.

The author was an instructor in Church Office Procedures at
Southern Baptist Theological Seminary. She writes this practical
book to assist pastors in being more efficient with their time and
energy. The book considers the common concern of church office
space, material and equipment.

MICKEY, Paul A. and Robert L. Wilson. *Conflict and Resolution.*
Nashville: Abingdon, 1973. 160pp.

This book uses case studies to examine the issues of conflict
between individuals and groups in the church. After a chapter on
the theological and psychological principles of conflict, there is a
series of short case studies with discussion questions designed to
highlight the basic issues involved. No decisions or solutions are
offered.

PETRY, Ronald D. *Partners in Creation: Stewardship for Pastor and People.* Elgin, IL: Brethren Press, 1980. 126pp.

This volume was designed as a text for a seminary course in stewardship. The first section treats the scriptural and theological dimensions of stewardship. The second section deals with the practical aspects from the point of view of the pastor. In one of the appendices, the author outlines a seven session study course entitled "a faith view of Stewardship". The author is a pastor of the Church of the Brethren.

PIERSON, Robert H. *So You Want To Be a Leader! A Spiritual, Human Relations and Promotional Approach to Church Leadership and Administration.* Mountain View, CA: Pacific Press Publishing Association, 1966. 152pp.

The author writes from his personal experience as an Adventist pastor and administrator, especially in Southern Asia. He has subtitled the book: A Spiritual, Human Relations, and Promotional Approach to Church Leadership and Administration. The emphasis has been placed on the spiritual aspects (scripture) and common sense approaches to administration.

POOVEY, W. A. *How to Talk to Christians about Money.* Minneapolis: Augsburg, 1982. 128pp.

This book is divided into two parts. The first discusses various aspects of stewardship. The second part contains short addresses on money based on various biblical texts. It is intended to assist the minister in speaking about money and stewardship.

RUDGE, Peter F. Ministry and Management. London: Travistock Publications, 1968. 191pp.

This book reflects the author's experience as a minister in the Church of England and his management studies. The first section describes five theories of administration and examines their theological implications. The next section investigates these same theories as they are practiced in ecclesiastical administration.

RUSH, Myron D. *Management: A Biblical Approach.* Wheaton, IL: Victor, 1983. 236pp.

This book is designed to provide the principles of management outlined in the bible. It also supplies the leadership and management tools needed to apply these biblical principles of management successfully. The author is the owner of a manufacturing firm and a consultant for business firms and christian organizations. He attemps to write for the christian businessman as well as the church leader. There is a chapter on team spirit, planning, decision-making, communication skills, delegation, time management, conflict, and the christian manager's role in society.

SAFRANSKI, Scott R. *Managing God's Organization: The Catholic Church in Society.* Ann Arbor., MI: UMI Research Press, 1985. 199pp.

This volume is the revision of the author's doctoral dissertation. It studies the Catholic Church from an organizational, not theological perspective. The focus is the interaction of units, at various levels of the church's hierarchy, with groups outside the church. Church organization and management processes are then studied in terms of adaptations made in an effort to assume cooperation and stable relationships with important internal and external interest groups and resource suppliers. The work contains the results of an empirical case study in which the resource dependence model was applied to one archdiocese.

SHAWCHUCK, Norman. *What It Means To Be a Church Leader.* Indianapolis: Spiritual Growth Resources, 1984. 71pp.

The author studies three topics from a biblical and theological perspective: appropriate ministry styles, the "seasons" which come to a congregation and the necessity of adapting one's ministry style according to the "seasons." The three topics of ministry found in the bible are priest, prophet and king. The author believes that each congregation today needs the same three ministry styles: priest, prophet and organizational leader.

STATON, Knofel. *God's Plan for Church Leadership.* Cincinnati: Standard Publishing, 1982. 155pp.

The author studies the biblical principles and corresponding practices that he judges are essential for effective christian leadership. The leadership of Jesus is explained. There are chapters on Paul, Barnabas, the apostles, the pastors, and the elders. The final chapters analyze the biblical findings.

SWINDOLL, Charles. *Leadership: Influence That Inspires.* Waco: Word Books, 1985. 72pp.

This small volume is a treatise on leadership from the biblical point of view. The author has searched the scriptures for the essence of leadership and the characteristics of both effective and ineffective leadership. The teaching of the bible is applied to the practical tasks of church leadership today.

SWINDOLL, Charles R. *Hand Me Another Brick.* Nashville: Thomas Nelson, 1978. 207pp.

This is a biblical treatise on leadership. Each chapter explores the scripture for examples of the theme being treated, e.g., training for leadership, motivation, discouragement, etc. These ideas were first given as sermons and lectures at leadership seminars.

Theology, News and Notes-Alumni Newsletter. Pasadena, CA: Fuller Theological Seminary, 1973. 23pp.

This little booklet reprints seven articles on the topic of management in the church which appeared in earlier newsletters. The authors are experienced and recognized experts. They explain their ideas in goal setting, priorities, planning and motivation.

THOMPSON, Thomas K., ed. *Stewardship in Contemporary Theology.* New York: Association Press, 1980. 252pp.

This book is an outgrowth of a Theological Study Conference on Stewardship held in 1979 at Wagner College in New York. The conference was sponsored by the National Council of Churches. The nine chapters of this volume are the presentations made during the conference. The topics are: stewardship in the bible, history of christian stewardship, the theology of stewardship, tithing, and ethics of stewardshipp.

VAN BENSCHOTEN, A. Q., Jr. *What the Bible Says about Stewardship.* Valley Forge: Judson Press, 1983. 96pp.

This is a study guide book. It is designed for five two-hour study groups and includes a leader's guide. The author, the associate director for World Mission Support of the American Baptist Churches, primarily focuses on the bible and its practical application in daily life. God has given us stewardship over the world's resources and this program assists people in understanding God's plan.

WALKER, Joe W. *Money in the Church*. Nashville: Abingdon, 1982. 125pp.

"I believe talking about money in the church is holy talk, deeply theological, and as sacred as prayer." So says the author of this volume which examines the part money plays in the United Methodist Church. He reports on the past and present patterns of giving. He studies the motivation used in collecting money and the motives which move Methodists to give. The book concludes with a discussion of the financial pressures facing the denomination and offers some methods to meet these challenges.

WALRATH, Douglas A. *Planning for Your Church*. Philadelphia: Westminster Press, 1984. 112pp.

This work describes ways and means of effective long-range planning within a congregation. The author uses a team approach and emphasizes basic planning which sets overall goals and fashions programs to accomplish the goals. After focusing on the minister's own style of leadership and the choice of the planning committee, he looks at the process of community analysis. He then shows how to establish priorities and achieve consensus for a plan of action. The author is professor of Pastoral Studies at Bangor Theological Seminary.

ZEHRING, John William. *Working Smart: A Handbook for New Managers*. Garrett Park, MD: Garrett Park Press, 1985. 78pp.

It is not enough to work hard, one must work smart. The author, vice-president of Bangor Theological Seminary, explains how to be a manager and survive not only in business but in ministry. He treats communication skills, computer skills, and methods of motivation. (from a review by Manfred Holck, Jr.).

CHAPTER ELEVEN

Time Management

ADAMS, Jay E. *Shepherding God's Flock.* Grand Rapids: Baker Book House, 1979. 530pp.

This is three books in one volume. The first section on pastoral life treats the practical questions about the ministry such as making house calls, visiting the sick, managing time, etc. The second section is on pastoral counseling. The third section is on pastoral leadership. In it the author discusses his views of authority, delegation, communication, planning, program design, finance and other administrative topics.

ASHEIM, Ivar and Victor R. Gold, eds. *Episcopacy in the Lutheran Church: Studies in the Development and Definition of the Office of Church Leadership.* Philadelphia: Fortress Press, 1970. 261pp.

This is a historical and theological study of the development and meaning of the office of leader in the Lutheran Church. By tracing historical lines and transitions over time and cultures, it attempts to give the younger churches of Asia and Africa some assistance in answering the questions about what must be held constant and what can be adapted to local conditions.

BANNON, William J. and Suzanne Donovan. *Volunteers and Ministry: A Manual for Developing Parish Volunteers.* New York: Paulist Press, 1983. 117pp.

This manual discusses many aspects of the relationship between the church and its volunteers. The authors deal with such topics as recruiting, training, supervising and evaluating volunteers. The last chapter is about time management and delegation. The work reflects the authors' year-long training program at a Catholic parish in Ohio.

BERGER, Hilbert J. *Time to Negotiate: Guidelines for Pastors to Follow When Salary Support is Considered.* New York: Friendship Press, 1973. 56pp.

This book was written for pastors who must negotiate their salaries with lay boards. The author, an experienced pastor, lays down the principles of such negotiation and outlines a method. While aimed as a tool for pastors, it also serves as a guide for lay committees.

BROWN, J. Truman. *Church Planning a Year at a Time.* Nashville: Convention Press, 1984. 24pp.

This booklet is a practical guide to church planning. It contains very little theory. There are numerous charts, timelines and questions which a planning group could use in its work.

CLAGETT, John Y. *Management for the Self-Governing Church.* Buffalo Grove, IL: J.Y. Clagett, 1983. 151pp.

Leaders in self-governing churches who are not confident with their role descriptions will find much practical advice in this book. It covers such topics as planning, budgeting, managing time, decision-making, motivation and training other leaders.

DAYTON, Edward R. *Tools for Time Management: Christian Perspectives on Managing Priorities.* Grand Rapids, MI: Zondervan, 1974. 192pp.

This book is a series of practical thoughts and suggestions on time management for the Christian church leader. Most chapters are no more than one page and are arranged alphabetically. The author envisions this resource as a tool box making these suggestions readily available to the reader.

DEEGAN, Arthur X. *The Priest As Manager.* New York: The Bruce Publishing Co, 1969. 154pp.

For this author the manager is the coordinator of the activities of others. The functions of a manager are planning, organizing, directing, motivating and controlling. This book aims to help the priest be more effective as an administrative leader. It discusses the process of management and the development of management theory. It explains the use of time, the art of delegation, styles of leadership, management by objectives and problem solving. The author concludes the book with a case study.

ENGSTROM, Ted W. and Edward R. Dayton. *The Art of Management for Christian Leaders.* Waco, TX: Word Books, 1976. 285+pp.

This book contains both theory and practice. It treats the question of the nature of christian leadership and how it differs from secular organizations. The authors, well known for their publications, write about planning, leadership skills, hiring staff and managing time, meetings and interruptions.

FLYNN, Leslie B. *How to Save Time in the Ministry.* Nashville: Broadman Press, 1966. 95pp.

"Work smarter not harder" is the motto of this practical booklet on efficiency. The author has gathered experiences and suggestions from pastors and other religious leaders. The chapters discuss such topics as delegation, planning ahead, scheduling, using spare minutes, starting earlier and taking time off.

HULME, William E. *Your Pastor's Problems.* Minneapolis: Augsburg, 1967. 165pp.

The pastor's problems with people, the church organizations and with himself are explored in this book. The ten chapters cover such topics as the need to succeed, the pastor's family, loneliness, use of time and living a balanced life.

LEAS, Speed B. *Time Management.* Nashville: Abingdon, 1978. 123pp.

This volume explains how church leaders must take the initiative if they are to be good stewards of the hours given by God to them. A good leader cannot passively accept the demands placed by others. The leader must set priorities and allocate time. The author does not simply list "oughts" but the "laws" to use time creatively and effectively. The compulsive worker and the procrastinator are described and used as case studies.

McCARTT, Clara Anniss. *How to Organize Your Church Office.* Westwood, NJ: Fleming H. Revell Co, 1962. 63pp.

The author was an instructor in Church Office Procedures at Southern Baptist Theological Seminary. She writes this practical book to assist pastors in being more efficient with their time and energy. The book considers the common concern of church office space, material and equipment.

POWELL, Luther P. *Money and the Church.* Chicago: Association Press, 1962. 252pp.

The author had two purposes in writing this book: to trace the various motives and methods throughout history of the christian church and to set forth some guiding principles for financing the church today. Part one discusses history up to the Reformation. Part two treats the church in early America. The last part focuses on the present time.

RUDGE, Peter F. *Management in the Church*. London: McGraw Hill, 1976. 172pp.

In the first section of this book the author establishes the relevance of management in the church. A case is made in each of the various fields of management (personnel, financial, property, household, office, time) and the case is argued on a very practical level. The second section describes new intiatives for restructuring the church, using examples from the Catholic Church. It is then demonstrated that this new church idiom bears close resemblance to management concepts found in the business world.

RUSH, Myron D. *Management: A Biblical Approach*. Wheaton, IL: Victor, 1983. 236pp.

This book is designed to provide the principles of management outlined in the bible. It also supplies the leadership and management tools needed to apply these biblical principles of management successfully. The author is the owner of a manufacturing firm and a consultant for business firms and christian organizations. He attempts to write for the christian businessman as well as the church leader. There is a chapter on team spirit, planning, decision-making, communication skills, delegation, time management, conflict, and the christian manager's role in society.

SCHALLER, Lyle E. *Survival Tactics in the Parish*. Nashville: Abingdon, 1977. 208pp.

The author envisions this book as a sequel to his 1973 THE PASTOR AND THE PEOPLE. This volume follows the same mythical Don Johnson as he completes a nine-year pastorate at St. John's Church. The first three chapters are intended to be a part of an education program as the pastor reflects on his career. The next two chapters are directed at a broader congregational audience and discusses the "signs" surrounding every church and the invisible reward system. The following six chapters are intended to stimulate congregational thinking about such issues as lay leadership, community image and goal setting. The final four chapters focus on the role of the pastor, this time from a joint congregational-ministerial perspective.

WHITE, Robert N., ed. *Managing Today's Church*. Valley Forge: Judson, 1981. 192pp.

This book comes out of five years of church management seminars held at the Babcock Graduate School of Management of Wake Forest University. The authors are seminar faculty members. They write about the fundamentals of management in a church environment. There is a chapter on the role and duties of the pastor. Planning is treated in three chapters (strategic, short-term and annual financial planning). After the chapter on marketing, three chapters follow on human resource management. The final chapter is on time management.

CHAPTER TWELVE

Volunteer Management

BANNON, William J. and Suzanne Donovan. *Volunteers and Ministry: A Manual for Developing Parish Volunteers.* New York: Paulist Press, 1983. 117pp.

This manual discusses many aspects of the relationship between the church and its volunteers. The authors deal with such topics as recruiting, training, supervising and evaluating volunteers. The last chapter is about time management and delegation. The work reflects the authors' year-long training program at a Catholic parish in Ohio.

HEUSSER, D. B. *Helping Church Workers Succeed: The Enlistment and Support of Volunteers.* Valley Forge, PA: Judson Press; 1980. 94pp.

No one denies the emphasis of volunteers in the history of our churches. This book helps churches take volunteerism and the volunteers more seriously. The author intends to treat the subject in a beginning fashion. He writes about theology, supervision, motivation, adult learning and evaluation. He concludes with a series of appendices containing forms and tables. The author is pastor of a Baptist Church in California.

JOHNSON, Douglas W. *The Care and Feeding of Volunteers.* Nashville: Abingdon, 1978. 125pp.

This volume offers a realistic and effective approach to the development and maintenance of church volunteers. The author's basic assumption is that a volunteer is a human being with real needs. He writes about the role of volunteers, identifying and recruiting volunteers, giving them assignments, planning with volunteers, running meetings and training volunteers. Dr Johnson is executive director of the Institute for Church Development.

United Church of Christ. *The Ministry of Volunteers.* United Church of Christ, Office for Church Life and Leadership, 1979.

This is a series of several booklets on the topic of volunteers in church ministry. The titles of each booklet are: 1. Volunteers and Volunteer Ministries; 2. The Church and Its Volunteers; 3. Guiding the Church's Volunteer Ministry Program; 4. Developing a Mission Statement; 5. Training Volunteers; 6. Supporting Volunteers; 7. Completing Volunteer Ministries. The series describes and resources a program for recruiting and developing volunteer ministries.

WIEST, Elam G. *How to Organize Your Church Staff*. Westwood, NJ: Fleming H. Revell Co, 1962. 63pp.

This book aims at helping the pastor become a more effective administrator of church staff. Consideration is given to both professional as well as volunteer staff. The author treats such topics as the purpose of church organization, planning, problem-solving, titles, job descriptions and evaluations.

WILSON, Marlene. *How To Mobilize Church Volunteers*. Minneapolis: Augsburg, 1983. 153pp.

The author, an international consultant on volunteerism, writes about the theory and practice of recruiting, managing and retaining volunteers. She explains the organizational structure and climate which fosters volunteerism. She then describes a plan which a church could use. She addresses the problems and offers fifty pages of helpful appendices.

Author Index